Tapestry
of
Tears

Tapestry
of
Tears

by

R D Payne

Paperback ISBN 1 904908 02-0

**Produced
by**

Central Publishing Services
Royd Street Offices
Milnsbridge
Huddersfield
West Yorkshire
HD3 4QY

www.centralpublishing.co.uk

Would I do it all again? I think not.

Did I really live through all that, or was it but a dream?

If I could change the way I've lived, what changes would I make?

Some things I had no control over, yet others were of my own making.

That old, well-known adage: 'Life is what you make it.'

Could this be true?

If so, where did I go wrong, and why so many tears?

Part I

TAPESTRY OF TEARS

It had all begun on a chilly October morning in a sleepy Yorkshire village on the edge of the Pennines. The Year was 1936. The peace of the morning was broken by the lusty cry of a newborn infant making its entrance into the world.

Ruth had arrived.

As the midwife wrapped the baby for the first time, the night's stars were fading and daylight was beginning to creep across the sky.

"Here you are, dear, you have a beautiful healthy daughter and judging by the noise she's making, she has a fine pair of lungs."

Many more tears were to be shed by Ruth in the life that lay ahead of her.

The autumn changed to winter, followed by spring. The child grew well and happy, going through the normal stages from baby to toddler with no problems. By the time Ruth was approaching her second birthday, her mother was heavily pregnant again.

September arrived with shortening days, falling leaves of russet and gold. The trees undressing for winter; cold, damp mornings; the musty smell of autumn all around.

The new arrival was eagerly expected any day. After a very difficult labour, baby number two arrived, along with severe complications. The mother began to haemorrhage badly, and despite enormous efforts from the doctor and midwife, sadly she gave up her struggle to live. She died with her newborn infant, a twin to the one born five minutes earlier.

Mr Briggs stood looking down at his dead wife in disbelief, and at the tiny mite beside her, who had not even gasped for breath. Fate had dealt him a bitter blow, robbing him of his wife and his children of their mother.

As the doctor handed him his second daughter, he expressed his sincere condolences at Mr Briggs' loss. The midwife had tears in her eyes.

"Mr Briggs, how will you manage?" she asked.

Ruth's father had no reply; too much had happened too fast to grasp the significance of it all.

He was left alone to bring up a child hardly two years old and a newborn baby, both now motherless, along with a son and daughter from his wife's previous marriage.

"Dear God," he exclaimed in his grief. "What am I to do?"

Mr Briggs was a forty-five year old man with steel grey hair that stood upright on top of his head. He was thin-faced, almost gaunt, with a hard mouth and cold blue eyes behind his thick horn-rimmed spectacles. His body was small and bony, giving him a half-starved appearance as if he needed a good meal inside him. He rarely smiled and he had a temper that erupted like dynamite at the slightest thing, yet he was well liked among his fellow workmates. Overnight, he changed into a man with such worries that he knew not which way to turn. The shock and disbelief at his predicament was clearly visible on his face.

A local garage had employed him for a number of years following his apprenticeship as a motor mechanic. Their showroom was full of grand expensive cars, which were Mr Briggs' pride and joy. He was very efficient at his job and loved to see the gleaming cars in the showroom when the wealthy customers came to purchase.

How could this man of considerable standing be expected to give it all up to care for his own two children, and the other two, by himself?

But fate decreed otherwise.

When he notified his deceased wife's family of her death, they snatched the elder children from him, much to his dismay, as the last words he had spoken to his wife were that he would keep the children together.

Ruth was terribly distressed as she watched her older half-sister and brother being carried bodily away amidst screams and tears.

Mr Briggs was left with Ruth as well as the new infant, and a lifetime of being responsible for their welfare whilst facing a time of terrible sadness and sorrow in his life. He had lost his soul mate at far too young an age, and at completely the wrong time for his children. He did not know how to cope with the situation.

He gazed down at the tiny infant with eyes that swam with sadness, his heart breaking. She was about to start her life without the tender care of a mother. No bond had been established; death had come too rapidly.

He was visibly shaken from the events of the last hours. The tension had mounted as the birth drew near, but he had certainly not expected such a dramatic turn of events. He had always been a strong-willed man in complete control of his life, now he was helpless to deal with the terrible consequences that followed the birth of this child. He had often been described as cold, his feelings and emotions rarely on display, but now he sat down, put his head in his hands - the weight of the burden almost too much to bear - and cried uncontrollably.

It was an impossible task for him even to contemplate the rearing of two children without a wife at the same time as trying to keep a job so that he had the means of providing everyday living expenses.

It was with the greatest reluctance that he had to contact the welfare home. There was no other way. With a very heavy heart, he spoke to the matron.

"Can you help me, please? I find myself in a terrible dilemma." He explained the circumstances of his wife's death and the situation in which he found himself.

"Certainly sir," came the reply. "I see no problem. We shall be happy to accept the girls at ten in the morning, if it is possible for you to make the necessary arrangements."

"Thank you, matron. It's a great relief to me to know that the girls will receive the love and attention they both need at this stage in their lives."

Mrs Smith, his next-door neighbour, had been attending to the children while he was away and she was awaiting his return.

"They've been little angels," she said. "No trouble at all. How did you get on at the welfare home? Are they willing to accept them?"

"Yes, Mrs Smith. They are to be ready for admittance at ten tomorrow."

"Oh good, that must be a load off your mind. You'll be able to visit, I suppose. I'll pop round at about eight thirty to give them some breakfast and pack some things for them, if you like. Can you manage until then?"

"Yes, thank you very much, Mrs Smith, that will be a great help. It's so kind of you - I don't know what I would have done without you."

At nine forty-five prompt the car arrived. An extremely bewildered Ruth was lifted into the car by her father whilst Mrs Smith took charge of her sister Elizabeth. The driver loaded the bags into the car, the sad-faced adults climbing in with them. During the journey, both children fell asleep. The car was warm, the silence broken only by the sound of breathing from Ruth as she slept. Both adults were unable to speak as they looked down at the sleeping children. *What will become of these tiny mites?* thought their father.

"This shouldn't be happening," he said at last to Mrs Smith, with tears in his eyes. He looked at her and saw that her own tears were very close, as she swallowed hard.

"You had no alternative, Mr Briggs" she finally said, regaining her composure. "You cannot be expected to care for them alone. What a tragedy it all is."

Ruth began her stay in the home with the other children. She was too young to understand this change in her life and soon adapted to having playmates. As the years passed by, she was herded together with dozens of others into huge crocodiles of children. They were grouped in pairs going along the road to school each morning; the same ritual taking place each evening, along with their minders.

Mealtimes were spent in the great hall with its beamed ceiling and dark grey painted walls. Large tables lined with benches were placed in rows, regimental fashion, each accommodating a dozen children on each side as they ate.

Sleeping arrangements consisted of huge dormitories containing beds lined up against the walls, each with identical, miserable-looking lockers and bedcovers.

The head minder, Mrs Bates, was an ogress of a woman in her late fifties, obviously ready for retirement. She had no patience with the children. She was as wide as she was long, with a round face and greying hair, eyes that were dark and piercing and a mouth that was hard and seldom smiling. She wobbled as she walked with heavy feet on the squeaky floorboards. When she spoke, a great booming voice came from her mouth, apparently rising up from her toes. Ruth and the other children were terrified of her. As soon as she entered, the room would fall silent. She wore a dark blue dress, buttoned up at the neck, with long sleeves buttoned at the cuff, making her hands look large and puffy. A white, heavily-starched apron fastened around her ample waist with a large bow. Her hair was fixed in a bun at the back of her head, on top of which was pinned a lace cap.

Ruth was fascinated by a large object that twinkled in the sunlight, standing against a wall in the great assembly hall. It was like a magical doorway into the unknown, and she watched the small girl performing before her. She spun and twirled, watching her image, totally engrossed in the movements before her. Giggling and laughing at the smiling face and shining eyes, she wondered where the little girl was. The girl must be hiding, so she decided to find her. Waiting until the room was quiet and she was alone, she squeezed and pushed her way into the small space behind. She found nothing, but with a thunderous noise, the object fell to the floor and shattered into hundreds of pieces that scattered in all directions.

Ruth stood shaking, so tiny and afraid, with the other children starting to cry. The sound of Mrs Bates' footsteps came scurrying into the room, her face scarlet with rage. Her eyes were wild, the bun on the top of her head bobbing up and down as she ran through the door.

"You wretched child! Now see what you have done!" she shrieked at Ruth, who by now was shaking from head to toe with fear, tears cascading down her bleached white face. She grabbed at Ruth's arm with her huge hand, the fingers biting into her skin. Pulling her almost off her feet, she dragged her down the length of the hall and along the corridor in front of the other children, who stood open-mouthed in silence.

"To the punishment room for you, you wicked child," hissed Mrs Bates, bundling her into the miserable room. Ruth sobbed uncontrollably. The walls were dark brown, wood-panelled with a small, barred window set high up to the right. The room contained nothing but a stool with a hard top, placed in the centre of the room. A single light hung from the ceiling without a lampshade. Roughly, Mrs Bates sat Ruth on the stool with a look that sent shivers down her spine.

"Stay there," was all she said as she slammed the door, leaving Ruth alone; a very frightened child.

As the daylight slipped away, the room grew darker and Ruth began to be more afraid. She needed the toilet, but no one came. She dare not shout for fear that Mrs Bates would arrive even angrier than before, so she sat silently and waited.

"Where's Ruth?" asked the tea lady, noticing her absence at the table

"Oh gracious me! I had forgotten the child," replied Mrs Bates. "She's in the punishment room."

The door was finally opened, allowing the light to stream in. Ruth ran to the tea lady, tears pouring down her face with relief.

"You must be the one that broke the mirror."

"Yes, miss, but I'm very sorry," replied Ruth.

The fear of the last two hours faded as she sat at the table for tea. She had learned a valuable lesson - not to break any more mirrors, ever, for fear of the wrath of Mrs Bates.

WAR

1936

The year of Ruth's birth was also a year of new beginnings; a new king, Edward VIII, was about to take the throne. But before his coronation he abdicated in favour of his brother George, the Duke of York, because of his love for the American woman named Mrs Simpson, a divorced woman. His brother became King in his place and was crowned George VI in 1937.

Sunday, September 3rd dawned bright after an Indian summer. Two days earlier, German troops had invaded Poland. An ultimatum had been issued to Germany: withdraw from Poland by 11 o'clock or we are at war. At 11.15, British Prime Minister Neville Chamberlain broadcast to the nation, consisting of 46 million citizens and the Empire, that Great Britain and Germany were at war.

During the King's Christmas speech, from the study in Buckingham Palace, the King spoke these solemn words:

"For the second time in the lives of most of us, we are at war." His broadcast ended with the words: "With God's help, we shall prevail, and may he bless and keep us all.

His grave message was broadcast to his shocked subjects at a time of harmony and family unity, when merriment should have prevailed.

Along with the war came shortages, rationing, Anderson shelters and gas masks. Most able-bodied men were enlisted in the war effort. Fathers, sons, and women all did their bit, the women taking over the jobs left vacant by the men who left to join the ranks of the fighting forces. Ammunition factories were working at full strength, mostly run by female workers. Air raids, barrage balloons and blackouts were everyday occurrences.

The war had an exceedingly traumatic effect on many places in England; wrecked homes, people killed and lives ruined. Many children were evacuated to safer places, away from the danger. Parted from their loved ones, they were bewildered and afraid. Food was in short supply and the black market flourished.

Many nights, Ruth was awakened from her slumber along with the other children. Gas masks - horrible things made of rubber and smelling peculiarly, shaped to fit over the child's face, half resembling a pig's snout which housed the respirator filter - were given to each child.

Together they trundled down to the air raid shelter in pairs in the usual crocodile, accompanied by the housemother from each dormitory. The younger children were put to bed first on makeshift bunks, whilst the older ones sat on anything that was available and wherever there was room. It was cold and miserable in the underground dens, but they were considered the safest place to be. Most of the younger children would cry themselves to sleep, not knowing what it was all about.

During that troubled time, Ruth was aware that her father began to visit. The war was now in its fifth year, and apparently nowhere near an end. Sometimes he would bring with him a happy-faced lady with translucent blue eyes that radiated laughter. She was five foot four and chubby, with medium-length light brown hair. Her skin was soft, with a delightful delicate perfume. The kindly lady would cuddle Ruth and talk to her in a soft, gentle voice, and she always brought some sweets with her.

Soon Ruth knew the meaning of love and she looked forward excitedly to their visits. Mr Briggs would pop his head around the door, saying to Ruth, "Guess who's here today?"

"Who, daddy, who?" she would ask excitedly, knowing full well whom to expect.

"Its mum! Are you happy to see her? "

"YES! YES! Daddy. Where is she?"

"Here I am, love."

Ruth, running as fast as she could on her little legs, fell happily into her arms.

"I've brought you some sweets today, but next time I shall not be able to bring any because I've used up all my coupons for this month."

The coupons were allocated to each family in the form of ration books. These contained small squares, and the shop assistant cut out the required amount for every item purchased. The adult sweet allowance for a month was 12oz (350 grams) each, every four weeks. Almost everything was rationed, including furnishings and clothing.

Mrs Bates, keeping her ever-watchful eyes on the children, bustled over to the three of them.

"Give me your sweets, Ruth, please. I will put them with the others until it's time for the share out, dear."

Sadly, Ruth handed her the packet, thinking that maybe, just maybe, she would get more of them than usual if she was lucky. So it was with everything; none of the children had anything that belonged solely to themselves, or that they could call their own. All the toys were shared between them; today it would be Jenny's, tomorrow Ruth's, and so on.

It took Ruth a number of years before she realised she had a sister. She overheard one of the housemothers talking to a small girl without hair, called Elizabeth, and ran over to her.

"Where's your hair?" she asked. "Your head is all purple."

Elizabeth, looking afraid, promptly burst into tears at the remark.

"There now! Ruth, see what you have done to your sister."

"Sister? What sister, miss?" Ruth asked anxiously.

The housemother looked puzzled.

"Dear God, child, don't tell me you didn't know you had a sister!"

"No, ma'am. No one ever told me she was my sister. Do I have any more?" Ruth asked.

"No child, just this one who you've made quite miserable at the moment, and I've been trying all morning to cheer her up. She didn't want her hair shaved off, but unfortunately she had ringworms so it had to go. The purple paint is to make sure they don't come back. Her hair will grow again quite soon, I assure you. It will most likely be a lot thicker, and maybe curly next time."

Ruth gave the small, miserable child a hug.

"Don't cry, Elizabeth," she said. "I'm so glad you're my sister. You must come and play with me every day. How old are you? I'm six."

"Four," came the timid reply from Elizabeth, who had stopped crying and was staring at Ruth with big red eyes.

"I go to school. Do you, Elizabeth?"

"No, not until next year when my hair has grown again. Do you like school, Ruth?"

"Yes," Ruth replied. "We can play in the sand and paint. I'm learning my ABC, and I can write my name. It's fun. "We have our dinner there. The teachers are nice and kind and we have lots of fun. You'll like it."

"Come along now, Elizabeth, we have to go. Ruth, you had better go and get ready for tea," said the housemother.

"Bye, Elizabeth," Ruth called, as she walked away to the washroom. "I know I'm going to like having a sister of my own."

Ruth was almost seven when she had her first experience of hospital. She awoke one Friday morning feeling very unwell. The housemother took one look at her and said, "Stay where you are, child, I shall have to fetch Mrs Bates."

When Mrs Bates arrived, she was accompanied by Dr Green, who solemnly declared she had scarlet fever. Mrs Bates looked on, her face set hard.

"She can't stay here," she said. "All the other children will get infected."

"Don't worry, I shall arrange for her to go into the local isolation hospital immediately," the doctor informed her.

"Thank you, doctor," Mrs Bates said with a weak smile as he left.

She glowered at Ruth, as if it was her own fault she was ill.

The journey was not very pleasant. Ruth's head ached and she could not stop shivering, despite the blankets that were piled on top of her. As Ruth was taken out of the ambulance, she saw a large Victorian building in front of her with glass corridors jutting out in all directions. Two nurses came to meet the ambulance, chattering to each other.

"Hello, dear, what's your name?" the blonde one asked with a smile.

"Ruth, ma'am," she replied, apprehensively.

"Don't worry, we shall soon have you feeling better love," said the other, patting her head gently. The huge doors swung open to reveal a long corridor and the entrance to Ward 3. Ruth was wheeled in and put into a separate cubicle.

"The doctor will be in shortly to assess you" she was told.

Ruth looked around the room. It was sparsely furnished with one bed, one chair and a locker. Different to her normal sleeping arrangements, it felt strange and very small as she was used to sleeping in a dormitory with 24 beds. Two walls were painted white, with windows reaching down to floor level on the other side to the right. On the left, a glass partition contained the door, which had shut behind the nurse as she left. Beside the bed, which Ruth was tucked into, stood a locker on which was a covered jug of ice and water. Beside it was a blue beaker turned upside down. Her clothes had been taken away in exchange for a thick white gown which felt rough on her skin.

Into the room stepped the doctor, wearing a mask and gown, which Ruth found a little frightening. After examining her, he confirmed what Dr Green had said: it was indeed scarlet fever.

"You'll have to stay in bed a few days, young lady," he told her. Ruth gladly accepted this news, as she felt so ill. Visitors were not allowed into the rooms for fear of cross-infection, but could stand outside the windows to talk.

After a week, a much-improved Ruth was approached by her blonde nurse.

"Your father came to see you yesterday," she said. "You were asleep, so we didn't disturb you. He did leave you a present, though. Would you like to have it now?"

"Yes please, nurse, what is it?"

"Oh, you'll have to wait and see. It's all wrapped up in a pretty parcel. I shall fetch it for you the next time I'm passing, but first I have to do a little job for Sister, or she'll be after me and then I shall be in trouble."

Ruth did not quite understand what she meant by her last remark, but smiled anyway and waited patiently for her return.

When she eventually got her present, which was wrapped in gaily-coloured paper with a beautiful bow, Ruth felt at it and discovered it was very soft. She excitedly tore the ribbon off and began to peel away the paper to reveal a hand-knitted golly with a huge smile, and big eyes that seemed to sparkle. Giving a squeal of delight, she cuddled it to her face.

"Ooh! It's beautiful," the nurse said as she looked at the happy face in front of her.

"Someone has spent a lot of time knitting this little fellow for you, Ruth. Look at his smart clothes, all bright, and what a lovely bow tie. I love his face - he looks almost real."

"Is he really MINE, nurse, or do I have to share him like the other toys at the home?" Ruth enquired hopefully.

"He certainly is yours, love, so you can keep him by your side in bed all the time. Give him a cuddle for me tonight before you go to sleep."

She left the room, closing the door gently and taking another look at the happy child before turning away with a lump in her throat, a tear almost escaping.

The days passed by pleasantly for Ruth, with her father and mum visiting as often as possible, although only able to talk through the window.

"How do you like your present, Ruth?" her father asked.

"He's lovely, *thank you* very much. He stays with me all the time except when I have a bath. He's so soft and cuddly. He sleeps in my bed and I talk to him."

Mr Briggs looked at mum and smiled.

"You'll soon be better and then you'll be able to go back to the home, love," mum said with a smile.

A tinge of sadness flashed in Ruth's eyes. "But I like it here. The nurses are so nice to me and I have golly. It's nice and quiet, and I can hear the birds singing every day when I wake up."

"But Ruth, dear, this is a hospital and other sick children will be waiting to come to be made better," her father told her. You will have to go back to the home when they say its time."

Five days later as the night nurse said goodbye to Ruth, she told her that Mrs Bates was coming in the morning. Ruth spent a restless night tossing and turning in her sleep, and as morning approached she awoke feeling quite sad.

"Good morning, Ruth, are you dressed?" the nurse asked as she came into the room. "If so, come with me to see sister, ready for your discharge." Ruth picked up her precious golly, but the nurse said, "leave him there, dear, I'll see to him. Hurry along now."

Ruth did as she was bid and followed the nurse along the corridor to the Sister's office.

The smiling sister was standing behind a large oak desk as they entered the room.

"Good morning, Ruth," she said. "It's nice to see you well and going home again. I hope you had a pleasant stay with us."

"Yes thank you, Sister," Ruth replied with a note of sadness in her voice.

"You've been a very good patient, Ruth, but now we must say goodbye. Mrs Bates is waiting for you at the front door. Give her this envelope straight away. Goodbye, my dear," Sister said as she ushered Ruth to the door with a smile, handing her over to the waiting nurse.

"Goodbye, Sister, and thank you," Ruth replied as she turned to leave. The blonde nurse took hold of Ruth's hand and led her gently through the swing doors, which closed silently behind them.

Ruth's feet dragged as if they were made of lead as she saw Mrs Bates approaching with a look of impatience on her face.

"Come on, child, I haven't got all day," was the sharp remark as Ruth passed the envelope Sister had given her into the outstretched hand. She followed Mrs Bates to the car and was told to sit on the back seat. She waved to the blonde nurse. Sadly looking round, she discovered to her dismay that the golly was absent. The car began to move away.

"Please, Mrs Bates," she begged, "I've forgotten my golly. Can we go back for him?" With her usual hard look, Mrs Bates turned to face her."

You cannot bring anything out of there, child. Don't you understand? It will be full of germs and shall have to be burnt."

"Burnt!" Ruth shouted in disbelief, the tears pricking her eyes. She began to cry hysterically.

"No, no, Mrs Bates. They can't do that to him! He's my friend, he made me better. Please stop the car, I have to fetch him."

"Now stop this tantrum this very minute, you naughty child!" was the only reply she received to her pleas as the car gathered speed, taking her further away from the hospital gates. Ruth was beside herself with grief and sobbed during the rest of the journey back to the home.

In her sadness, Ruth mourned for her lost friend. She went off her food, talked very little and slept restlessly, crying so many tears for her beloved golly.

HOME

War was still progressing through Europe, getting worse day by day. The housemothers were forever discussing it in small groups with hushed voices and solemn faces. The teachers at school stood huddled together, out of earshot of the children, discussing it all.

One particular cold winter's morning, with the snow falling like confetti and turning the playground into a fairyland, the headmistress assembled the children together in the hall.

"Now, children, I have some sad news to tell you. Jimmy Tate will not be at school for a few days. His daddy has been killed in the war. I want you all to promise me that you will be very kind to him when he comes back."

Some of the older children began to cry. Ruth wondered why her daddy had not gone to the war; most of the children at school had dads who were soldiers or sailors. She had no comprehension of the mass slaughter and atrocities being carried out against the Jewish population by the Nazis.

No one really knew the extent of it until after the liberation had taken place, years later. Terrible things were happening to people, things that could not be explained to children. Families everywhere were torn apart by evacuations; deaths of loved ones; messages of sons, fathers, husbands and sweethearts killed or missing in action. Homes were blown apart by bombs dropped from the skies.

It was a horrendous time, but people united in the common belief they had been taught in Sunday schools and churches about God's will. They had to accept so many things for which there was no sense or reason. Lives were changed in many different ways; some small, some drastic. It was all out of their control, yet time continued to pass by. Air raids with the constant whine of sirens; wardens' whistles; blackout; darkness everywhere until the exploding bombs detonated, causing devastation all around, lighting up the sky; fires starting up in piles of rubble that not ten minutes before had been someone's home.

It was during this troubled time that Mrs Bates sent for Ruth. After sitting her down in the large brown leather chair which stood in front of her desk, she told Ruth,

"You and your sister are going home. Your parents are coming for you tomorrow morning at nine-thirty."

Ruth's mouth gaped and her eyes registered amazement.

"Home..." she said, "Mrs Bates, where's Home?"

"Don't ask me, child, I don't know. You will have to wait and see for yourself tomorrow. Run along now and join the others."

At nine-thirty prompt, the two extremely excited girls were sitting in reception awaiting their parents. They saw their father and mum arrive in a blue car.

"Hello, girls," said Mr Briggs. "Are you ready? Mum is waiting for you both."

Ruth took hold of Elizabeth's hand.

"Come on, little sister," she said. "We are going...Home."

Home seemed to be miles away from the orphanage, which indeed it was - on the other side of town, in fact, which at that time of day was very busy with early-morning shoppers going about their business. On leaving the town, their journey took them through the suburbs out onto a long, winding stretch of road and into the countryside

The girls gazed in wonderment at the open fields with animals in groups, grazing in the emerald green grass. The sun cast shadows through the trees, making patterns in the fields, as fluffy white clouds drifted aimlessly across the great expanse of blue sky. They stared in wonder at the images unfolding in front of them, never seen before except in picture books.

As they travelled along, the road stretched in front of them and the farms were not as close together as before. There was nothing to see but green fields on either side until they reached a steep hill. The trees became much denser, making it almost dark. As they turned a corner, a small row of terraced houses came into view. Each house looked identical but for the different lace curtains hanging in each window. They were stone-built with black slate roofs; each one had two windows upstairs, plus a door and window beneath.

A few steps led to the entrance of each of them. These were either white or yellow, having been scrubbed clean and scoured with a donkey stone, which was the fashion of the time - a housewife's weekly job if her home was to be kept in order. Flower baskets hung down from the walls, creating a lovely picture for the excited girls.

"Here we are at last," Mum said, giving a soft chuckle at their flushed faces and sparkling eyes.

"Which is ours?" Ruth asked.

"The last one, next to the wood. You'll have plenty of room to play there."

Ruth giggled at Elizabeth.

"It's lovely in the spring when the trees are coming into bud, and nice and shady in the hot summer sun. We get lots of birds singing in the trees and building their nests. You'll be quite safe away from the road."

The car stopped outside number four. The girls were eager to explore their new surroundings.

"It's lovely, mum. Can we go into the wood and have a look round?" pleaded Ruth.

"All right, then. Two minutes while dad and I open the door and put the kettle on for a cup of tea."

"Come on, Elizabeth, let's go and play."

Together they ran into the wood, Ruth in front with Elizabeth running after her with squeals of delight.

Ruth felt she was going to burst, she was so happy as she ran through the trees with feet like feathers.

"We can have so much fun here, Elizabeth. No more Mrs Bates shouting at us."

Together they shouted 'Hooray!" at the tops of their voices.

"Let's go look in the house, Elizabeth," Ruth urged, after running round in the wood for a while. "We can play in the wood later."

Ruth, standing on her tiptoes, slowly opened the door to number four. This was the first glimpse that she could remember of the interior of a house. It all seemed so small to her - she was used to large rooms - but oh! how cosy it all looked.

In the large black fireplace, which towered over her head, a log fire was burning cheerfully in the grate. Its flames jumped upward to the chimney, creating a brightness that lit up the whole room. To the right was a door, and a long shelf stretched across the fireplace, level with the top of the door.

Looking to the back of the room, Ruth saw a square table with chubby legs, a chair tucked under each side. On the table was laid a pretty lace cloth on which stood a vase of flowers. Sitting on each chair was a soft padded cushion. To the left of the room was the window, opposite which was a sideboard with a huge radio in the centre. Between the fireplace and table was a settee, and two armchairs were in position facing the fire.

Beside the fireplace on the other side to the door, were cupboard doors in a recess. Ruth watched her mum walk over and open the door to reveal a large stone sink with a water tap over it.

"What's that door for, mum?" Ruth asked, pointing to the one on the right of the fireplace.

"You must be very careful when you go to that door, both of you. It leads to the cellar. Come with me and I'll show you."

She opened the door fully to lead the way for the girls down the steep stone steps. There was nothing much to see for the effort except a large stone slab and a peculiar gadget with rollers and a wheel, which mum told her she used on washdays. Alongside this was a tub and rubbing board. A few tools lay on the stone slab and a long, zinc bath hung on the wall. The cellar was painted white. It smelled funny and felt very cold.

Ruth remarked on the coldness to her mother, who told her the reason for it was to keep food fresh during the summer.

"That reminds me," said mum, "I have to visit the farmer today to see if he can let me have some eggs and bacon now I have two more hungry mouths to feed. It's very difficult to get fresh food with this war going on, but he has been most helpful and promised to try."

Rationing meant that families had to scrimp and scrape to save on food; they were allowed very little. Only two ounces of butter and cheese per person were allowed, plus one or two eggs.

These meagre rations did not go very far. Dried eggs could be obtained in packets every four weeks, but only one packet. You could get margarine or cooking fats if you were lucky; four ounces of each. Two ounces of tea were available, and eight ounces of sugar plus four ounces of bacon or ham. Each adult was allowed two or three pints of milk a week as well as a supplement of dried milk in a packet, one per person every four weeks. Vegetables, fruit and fish were not rationed, but were extremely scarce. Sweets were available at three ounces a week.

The result of the shortages was that people bought on the thriving black market anything that was available, but had to pay exorbitant prices after queuing for hours.

"Come along now, girls, let me show you where you're going to sleep," mum said, as she led them once more up the stone steps from the cellar. She closed the door behind them and firmly locked it.

Dad smiled at the girls as they passed him, heading for the stairs to lead them to the bedrooms. The girls followed mum up the red-carpeted stairs.

"This is where dad and I sleep, and next to our bedroom is where you will both be sleeping," mum informed them.

Ruth ran ahead of her, impatient so see her room. Pushing the door gently open, she gave a squeal of delight at the two beds standing side by side. Both were covered with pretty, floral bedspreads. The window curtains were made in the same fabric, giving the room a summer feeling; cheeriness she had not experienced before.

Pictures of small animals hung on the walls beside each bed and a fluffy rug lay on the floor, which was covered in pink linoleum.

"Do you like your bedroom?" mum asked of the girls, to which they answered in chorus,

"Yes, mum!"

By this time, Ruth was feeling that this is what heaven must truly be like.

WINTER

Alice had only recently married Ruth's father against the wishes of her family, who thought he was not a suitable partner for her given that he already had the two children from his previous marriage. Alice was the eldest of a family of four - two brothers and one sister - none of whom was married. Her father had died many years before, leaving her mother to rear the family alone. Her mother had tried on numerous occasions to persuade Alice to forget this man of whom she greatly disapproved, hoping she would meet a more pleasant person without ties. Alice was, however, determined to rescue the two small girls from the home, and against her family's wishes she married Mr Briggs.

A quiet, gentle lady, wanting very little from life except a decent home and family, Alice found herself responsible for two young girls for the first time in her life. Both girls looked undernourished and were small and skinny, with legs and arms like matchsticks. They were both desperately in need of tender loving care, which she vowed to herself she would give them to the best of her ability. Alice felt so sorry for her two charges, whose lives up to that point had not been easy.

She learned to love them as her own, making a decision that she would do her best not to conceive so that she could devote all her love and care to Ruth and Elizabeth.

Alice took great pleasure in purchasing the girls pretty new dresses and shoes. The girls loved the new clothes, having spent all their previous lives in regulation uniforms at the home. Their hair was washed and brushed tenderly before being plaited, and pretty ribbons were added to complete the finishing touch. Their contentment showed in their happy faces and twinkling eyes.

Home-cooked meals lovingly made by Alice began to fill out the hollows in their cheeks. The smell of cakes pervaded the home on a regular basis after Alice had spent hours in her small kitchen area, beating the mixture while the girls were at school. Each time they returned to the house they were greeted with motherly words and concern for their well-being.

It was heaven for the girls as they played in their own wood beside the house, wrapped in warm woolly scarves, hats and gloves. They each had a new padded coat to keep out the cold winter wind that whipped round the trees, making their cheeks glow.

But it certainly did not feel like heaven for Alice, their mum. Coal was almost non-existent and logs for the fire were too expensive to buy, if you could get any at all.

Mr Briggs was still working as a motor mechanic in the town. The girls rarely saw him during the week. He left early in the mornings and arrived home late at night after they were in bed. The local bus service left a lot to be desired; on disembarking at the bus terminus, he then had to walk two miles before he reached home.

Usually, on his return he would wash at the kitchen sink before eating his prepared meal, and then fall asleep in his armchair beside the blazing fire.

Alice spent the days at home, using her time after the children had left for school in chopping wood that father had sawn from the trees at weekends. The sight of her hands with open cuts, bleeding where the branches had scratched and blistered her, made Ruth wince every time she saw her mother walking in with her arms full of logs.

"Poor mum! Look at your hands again – they're so sore," she often said.

"Never mind, love, they'll soon get better. We can have a nice warm house for daddy when he comes in. I think it's going to snow. I can feel it in the air; it's quite nippy outside tonight."

The mornings were frosty as the windows in their small house faced to the north, catching the cold biting winds during the night. Each morning the girls inspected their bedroom window to see the pattern Jack Frost had made while they were tucked up snugly in their beds. He was an exceptional artist during the night, creating his masterpieces for all to see. Beautiful patterns were displayed each morning on the glass window, twinkling in the weak morning sun.

Some mornings he had been too heavy-handed, making it impossible to see through the glass unless they melted the frost with their warm breath to create a peephole.

To keep the girls warm on their long walk to school, which was three miles across farming areas, dad had his own recipe: a spoonful of Compo, a mixture that taste slightly of liquorice. If added to warm milk, it created a satisfying glow inside the body. The girls loved it, so had no complaints about taking a daily dose.

Dad added a drop of whisky to his tea every morning to give him the same glow. A bottle lasted him quite a while, as he never drank at any other time.

The doctor lived quite along way away, so home remedies were frequently used. A spoonful of sulphur taken along with cod liver oil and malt was a weekly potion administered to all each week. For tummy upsets, camomile flowers were brewed like tea and drunk at regular intervals until the patient recovered. It tasted foul and the children hated it, so it was quite a battle to get it down and involved nose-holding and tears.

These home remedies paid off well, as neither of the children was absent from school, even though they were both very small in stature.

The cooking in the household was done in the side oven or on a small gas ring on the hearth. Alice would put some water in a small pan to heat quickly on the gas ring each morning to make the cup of tea or warm the milk for Compo.

One particular morning, the girls were getting ready as usual for school. Ruth bent down to tie her shoelaces as Alice bent to pick up the boiling water. In a split second they both stood up at the same time, Ruth catching the contents of the pan over her head. She screamed as the scalding liquid ran over her head and down her face and neck. Alice was distraught, but kept her wits about her. The local farmer had just delivered their morning milk supply in a bucket as he usually did, straight from the farm. It was ice cold. She grabbed Ruth and dunked her headfirst into the milk, making the child scream even louder. By then the three of them were crying; Elizabeth with fright, Ruth with shock and Alice with a look of horror on her face.

Each morning the girls were in the habit of loitering on their way to school. It was a long, tiring walk to get there along the roads that circled the farms. There were so many things to see: cows lifting their heads to see what the giggling was all about, gazing curiously with their big brown doleful eyes; flocks of birds circling round the fields, an occasional crow scattering them in all directions; daisy chains to make and hang around each other's necks.

They were such happy, carefree times, full of laughter.

They had been late so often that the teachers were surprised if they actually made it on time, so they had given up expecting them on the dot. Ruth liked school, so on this occasion after her tears had subsided and the cold milk had eased the burning sensation, she was ready to go.

"You can't go today, love," said mum, her face streaked with tears.

"I'll be all right now, mum, it feels much better. Please let me go."

With reluctance Alice let her go, but worried what the teacher would say about her as a mum.

The teacher, looking at the small, pigtailed head and very red face appearing through the door, late as usual, ran over to her.

"Whatever have you done to your face, child?" she asked.

Ruth explained about the mishap, telling her that mum had not wanted her to go to school that day. "But it's painting day today and I really wanted to come; I like painting, miss."

The teacher, on seeing that Ruth was quite happy to stay, let her remain there and do her painting. She kept a watchful eye on the girl, making sure that she was not in too much distress with her face, which as time passed grew redder and redder but did not seem to trouble her too much. The outcome of it all was that Ruth's face healed without scarring due to Alice's quick actions with the milk; it did not have time to blister.

Other childhood troubles were encountered, such as a cold, a cut or a tumble leading to a graze, but nothing drastic. Life continued, and the children grew happier by the minute.

'Evil seems to flourish in this world of sin and strife
But look beneath the surface at the deeper things of life
The mysteries of love with its blind suffering and sacrifice
Though everywhere we see the blindness and brutality of man
In all his ways, the torment and the terror, of these modern war-torn days
Turn from fear and folly let your prayers of faith ascend
Wait, and know that God will conquer in the end.'

Patience Strong.

OVERLORD

The beginning of the end of World War Two was launched from ports off the south coast of England on June 6th 1944.

The operation was to be called 'OVERLORD.'

The allied invasion consisted of a daring campaign involving the Army, Navy and Air force in an attempt to liberate Europe. Five assaults were planned on the Normandy beaches, a combined effort by American, British, French and allied troops.

Many tense hours were to pass before news came that the operation had been a success.

On July 20th 1944, German officers attempted to assassinate Hitler after their defeat. This attempt was unfortunately not a success.

The allied forces began to feel more confident that the end was in sight. But Hitler, in a ruthless gamble, achieved surprise by launching a counter-attack in the Ardennes. The American troops stood firm at Bastoyne, which became known as the 'Battle of the Bulge.'

In the Christmas of 1944 the allied troops were looking to cross the Rhine, the last great defence of the Third Reich, then on to victory.

After these events, more horrors were to be revealed when the Allies discovered the concentration camps, where Jews and prisoners of all nations had been systematically starved, tortured, experimented on and killed.

35 million souls had perished, 6 million of them Jews. In total, 10 million had been sent to Nazi concentration camps during the war, that had lasted five and a half years.

Victory in Europe day was designated a public holiday. It fell on the May 8th 1945, and was named V E Day for future generations.

"TODAY WE GIVE THANKS TO GOD FOR A GREAT DELIVERANCE. GERMANY, THE ENEMY WHO DROVE ALL EUROPE INTO WAR, HAS FINALLY HAS BEEN

OVERCOME."

This joyous message from the King sent the whole of his subjects into a frenzy of happiness.

Bunting, music, lights, joy everywhere - the elation was infectious.

"It's over!" was the ecstatic cry on everyone's lips. People united in joy, some laughing, some on their knees thanking God. At last there was peace.

BETTER DAYS

Ruth was eleven years old in 1947. The family had moved house a little nearer to civilisation and she had more friends to play with, spending many happy hours in her neighbour's garden with their children.

She had developed a fascination for frogs, much to the dismay of Alice. Putting the linen away one day, Alice discovered to her horror where Ruth was putting them when she brought them home in a matchbox. Two frogs escaped, jumping around the bedroom, to the wild shrieks of Alice, bringing the girls running in to see what the matter was.

"Take them out this minute!" was her irate command, when she got over her fright.

Catching them, however, was a different matter. It was quite a task, with the three of them crawling round on hands and knees over the bedroom floor. One hour later, having finally succeeded, the giggling girls took them back to the garden next door with a very stern warning not to bring any more into the house from a very angry mum.

Life at the new house became easier for all. Gone were the days when a visit to the loo was like an arctic expedition: round the block, across the yard in a howling gale, climbing over thistles, torch in hand, covered in goose pimples. The old loo had a freezing wooden seat over a tub of strongly-smelling San-Izal, and not a drop of water to be seen anywhere. In wet weather the raindrops fell on one's head as they sat, and icy winds blew around feet and other regions exposed to the elements.

The council wagon called monthly to empty the tub of its deposits, the stench from which was revolting.

Thank goodness for the enamel pail Alice kept under the sink for emergencies during the night, which she emptied dutifully first thing each morning.

Gone also was the zinc bathtub from the cellar, replaced by a bathroom complete with bath, toilet, hand basin and best of all, hot running water. No more ladling buckets of used water out of the bath, which took ages and was back-breaking work - bliss.

Instead of gaslight with gossamer-thin mantles that disintegrated at the slightest touch, they had electric light.

At the house next to the wood, the radio had been operated by the use of an accumulator battery that contained acid. Every so often, depending on how much it was used, Dad had to take it to be recharged. This was a nuisance, as well as the radio being ugly to look at and very cumbersome.

The sheer luxury of switching on the electric radio was a pleasure for dad, as you could tell by the smile on his face. He sang and whistled along with Vera Lynn to the songs made famous by her during the war. His favourite ones were: 'The white cliffs of Dover' and 'We'll meet again.'

Vera had been known all the war years as the 'Forces' Sweetheart.' She had sung with great feeling the words that became engraved on many hearts. Gracie Fields was another of his favourites. Her strong Rochdale voice singing 'Wish me luck as you wave me goodbye,' was a tearjerker every time it was heard. There were many others, all appropriate for the time.

ENSA had been formed to entertain the troops and the workers in the factories who made munitions. Concert parties organised by the group consisted of comedians, singers, dancing girls, magicians - anyone who could entertain and take peoples' minds off the dreadful time.

Men and women all joined in to try and keep up morale. What destiny life had in store for many in their audiences was unknown even to themselves. Their songs lingered on many years after the war, etched into peoples' subconscious minds, easily reborn at the least reminder.

At the house, a coal fire burned cheerfully in the grate. This time it was real coal, delivered to the house weekly. The flames created a mirage of pictures as they flickered, having a soothing effect on the watcher. All was bliss at the Briggs household - or was it?

As winter approached the nights turned colder and the days shortened; the winds blew colder and stronger.

"We're in for a bad one this year lass," said dad, as he arrived home from work one cold blustery evening. "I can feel it in my bones - the wind fair blows through ya," he said, shivering from head to toe.

"Oh dear, I hope not," replied Alice with a worried expression on her face. "I hate the wintertime; it's so bleak living out here. Do you think it will snow a lot?"

"I hope so," the girls chorused together. "We can build a snowman then."

It started very gently at first, like May blossom falling from the trees in the strong wind. Soon the flakes began to get bigger and faster. In no time at all, it covered everything in its path, transforming all into a bright white scene of pure delight, as if the clouds had fallen from the sky dressing the earth in swansdown.

"If it carries on like this all night, we shall have to dig ourselves out in the morning, lass."

On hearing dad's remarks, the girls began skipping around with glee.

"I hope it does," Ruth said to Elizabeth, much to Alice's dismay.

Snow it did, all night, and the following day and night also. The winds were blowing very strongly, creating drifts up to seven feet deep. The walls around the fields disappeared completely under its heavy mantle. Everything was covered in the fluffy white down. The electric pylons stood erect but the wires were weighted down, double their normal thickness, humming a tune as anyone passed.

The farmers were out every day, hour after hour, with tractors and snowploughs, trying their level best to keep the road clear to the shop and plodding on to the animals cut off in the fields.

A hush descended on the area late at night, with everyone

exhausted with his or her efforts. It was so quiet after the noise of the day, one could almost hear a fairy sing.

Alice had made an appointment for the girls to be immunised before the snow had begun. Now she looked out of the window before exclaiming with dread,

"However shall we get there?"

"We'll walk," chorused the girls together.

"But you have no Wellingtons. You have your clogs – they'll help you grip the snow - but your legs will be wet through." Then mum had an idea. "We shall use your dad's socks – they'll look funny but who cares, your legs will keep warm. First a good dose of Compo, for all of us."

Within the hour, they were off, mum with a large bag of socks tucked under her arm. The girls walked along with mum, all laughing at themselves. Slowly they trudged through the snow, the wind turning their cheeks cherry red. At first it was fun, but soon it made their legs ache.

"Shall we soon be there?" asked Ruth, her knees beginning to chafe, wishing she were sitting near a nice cosy fire warming her toes.

"We shall sing a little song," mum replied. "It will help us on our way." And she began singing: 'She'll be coming round the mountain when she comes, when she comes, she'll be coming round the mountain when she comes. She'll be wearing silk pyjamas when she comes. Old MacDonald had a farm, E.I.E.I.O. And on his farm he had a dog, E.I.E.I.O.'

And so it continued, the singing and the laughter that accompanied it, helping the three weary travellers on their way. Socks were changed at regular intervals, making mum's bag heavier each time.

Eventually they arrived at the surgery and the doctor was amazed to see the three of them.

"I never expected to see you today, Mrs Briggs," he exclaimed with surprise. "However did you get here?"

"We walked," they sang together, laughing.

"Right girls, let's get you seen to. Come with me into the surgery and we'll get this job done with as soon as possible, then you can be on your way before it gets any worse."

Mrs Briggs sat down heavily on the nearest chair, glad of a rest. *I must have been mad to contemplate this journey today,* was the thought that passed through her mind as she sat sorting out more dry socks for the girls on their return. Within five minutes they were back with her, their vaccinations complete.

"Would you like to come and sit by the fire for a while and have a cup of tea?" the doctor asked mum, looking at her exhausted face.

"Yes please, doctor, I'd like a chance to get warm, thank you for asking," she replied gratefully," but we shan't have to be long, as it's a very long way back and I think it may snow again."

With a nice warm glow inside, the three of them set off on their journey home with fresh socks and rested legs, happy to be on their way home. They began to sing again: 'Old MacDonald….'

Well recovered the next day, the girls looked out of their window to see that more snow had fallen during the night. This time, however, it had covered everything. On opening the door with great difficulty, dad was greeted by a snowdrift which promptly fell on top of him, turning him into a snowman.

The girls and mum laughed so much that they ended up huddled in a heap, practically hysterical, so much so that dad had to eventually laugh along with them.

After a breakfast of a steaming hot dish of porridge with melted treacle swimming round in the middle like a mini whirlpool, they all donned coats, scarves, woolly hats and gloves to tackle the mammoth task of snow-moving. Accompanied by numerous cups of tea and compo, the backbreaking shovelling job was done.

The farmer with his tractor had cleared a path to the road earlier, which reminded mum she needed to go to the farm.

"I need some eggs to pickle," she said.

"Can we come with you?" asked the girls.

"All right then," she replied with a smile, "but hurry up - I can't wait all day for you two."

The farm was a twenty-minute walk away, up the hill and round the corner, past the local public house, up the lane to the right. As they got to the corner, a magnificent sight came into view. The public house and the area around it had been transformed into an arctic wonderland. In front of them stood the unusual sight of a giant igloo, a passage cut through the middle to the door of the pub. The three of them gazed in wonder at this miracle of nature before their eyes.

"How lovely," mum remarked, looking at the speechless girls, who stared with eyes wide-open in disbelief.

Winters were usually terrible, with miles and miles of snow-covered fields and bitter winds, and freezing cold biting deep into hands, feet and faces. Chilblains were quite common every year; hot, burning, itching blotches on hands and feet. Mum's favourite cure for them was to walk barefoot in the snow. After the initial shock of cold, the relief was instantaneous.

Many villages were isolated in the winter wonderland, pretty on the eyes, with trees taking on a different look with their branches heavily laden with snow. Roads were blocked by huge drifts created by winds during the night. Houses had beautifully-patterned windows, etched personally by Jack Frost on his nightly calls.

The farmer had plenty of eggs, also some lovely home-fed bacon, for which mum was very grateful. She had some way of preserving the eggs for later use. They were put into large earthenware pots along with a special liquid, and left for a number of weeks before being used.

That particular winter, the snow had been especially heavy. When the thaw eventually came, it brought with it other problems. The drains were unable to take the sheer volume of water that ran down the roads like rivers.

One morning mum became very agitated. On going down to the cellar, she found her precious eggs floating like mushrooms on a lake in the water that was slowly filling up the cellar.

The bedroom ceiling had sprung a leak as the snow melted on the roof outside, bringing the slates off. Then it started to rain and water cascaded into the bedroom through the hole.

Buckets and bowls were hastily put into place to catch the offending water, which began to play tunes as it fell into the receptacles.

As the winter turned to spring, it was obvious that other things were not quite right. Mum had a permanent frown on her face; Dad was getting worse-tempered by the day. He was often swearing, much to mum's annoyance, and he smoked far too many Woodbines for mum's liking.

On numerous occasions Ruth found her mum having a little weep to herself as she went about her daily chores. On enquiring why, she was told her dad had a lot of worries, which were making him bad tempered.

Not many months passed before the family was on the move again. The furniture was loaded into a van in double-quick time, with no explanation to the girls.

The new house was in a more densely-populated area; much smaller and not as modern as the last. Gone was the bathroom - once more an outside loo - but thankfully it was in the garden this time.

The house was situated in a long terrace of back-to-back houses. It was the end house, through a passage with great iron doors, behind number twenty. There was a small garden with a large stone wall running down to the right of it, on which a few climbing shrubs were creeping upwards, ready to burst into leaf.

A small lawn was in the centre, with a border on three sides. A flagged path ran down to the loo and dustbin area. The view from the house was not very interesting, for it consisted of other houses and gardens, some very overgrown with weeds. It all seemed dark and drab, with not much chance of any sunlight creeping through between the houses. It was miserable compared to the beautiful countryside they had been used to for so long.

Another shock awaited the girls; mum had found a job and was to start work in two days' time. Alice was to be employed as a shop assistant in the town in a china shop, a ten-minute bus ride away from home. School was a ten-minute walk away, but across the busy main road that led to town.

There were to be no more fields with cows pleasantly grazing near hedgerows full of chirping birds to cheer them along their way as before. They were all gone.

The house was much smaller also, the door opening straight into the sitting room, beyond which a door led to the small kitchen.

"Too small to swing a cat in," as dad would say, and with only two bedrooms this time.

From the kitchen, stone steps led to a small coal cellar. The house was hardly bigger than a dolls' house compared to the one they had just left, in Ruth's opinion. Would dad now be in a better temper and mum lose her frown? She pondered.

After a number of weeks, Elizabeth and Ruth settled into the new way of life, with more playmates and more going on around the area.

Mum liked her new job in the town and a happier atmosphere settled on the Briggs household.

The girls were allocated jobs to do around the house with instructions from mum on how to do them, to stop them getting up to mischief while waiting for her to come home.

They took turns with the washing up after the evening meal. One or the other helped with the ironing, while the other dusted the bedrooms. Mum found a little time to bake cakes on an evening sometimes. She was an excellent cook. Her cakes tasted delicious, so scrumptious, especially the ones with butter cream in that melted in one's mouth.

Some days, mum would be late in from work, especially when the deliveries of stock were due. The girls had to prepare their own tea then. They learned how to cook easy things like toast, egg, bacon and beans.

Dad seemed to spend a lot of time working over, so he took sandwiches, which had to be prepared in the evening.

Things soon began to pick up. Mum began to buy little things that took her fancy, the first of these being a beautiful china tea set that was her pride and joy. It was to be used when someone came to tea, which was not very often. She liked delicate things, especially china roses that she dotted around the house.

Ornate teapots became another obsession of hers. Small cottages with tree trunk handles and Toby jug faces appeared as if by magic, never meant to hold tea at all, much to Dad's annoyance. He forgave her eventually, for he knew she had to work very hard for the money she spent on her treasures, as she called them.

As the summer evenings grew longer, after doing their chores the girls were allowed to play with the neighbourhood children. The favourite game, enjoyed by all was 'tin can squat,' a very noisy game, much to the annoyance of the neighbours who were trying to watch their televisions.

One child was chosen to kick the can as far as they could while the other children went to hide. The one left behind had then to find them all and replace the can before it was kicked again.

Many happy hours were spent doing this until mum bought them both a whip and top, along with a box of chalks. Pretty patterns were drawn on the top, which was made of wood. The whip had a leather string tied to the handle, which was then wrapped round the top and placed on the floor. The whip was tugged hard to release it, making the top spin. With careful whipping the top could be kept spinning for quite a long time. The art of this was to make the prettiest patterns and keep the top spinning for the longest time.

Skipping was another pastime enjoyed by all, either solo or in teams. Many rhymes were invented for the team's skips and sung together as the girls took their turn in the centre of the rope.

It was all good exercise, costing very little for hours and hours of happy healthy fun.

TEENS

Nothing much different happened before Ruth reached her teen years. It did not seem long before she had to leave school to start her working life. She began in a shop that sold sewing machines and accessories.

She was still a very timid girl in adult company, finding it very difficult to approach customers as they came into the shop. She did, however, receive instruction on how to use the various sewing machines for the purpose of demonstrating them to prospective buyers. The finer points of new machines, which were a great improvement on older ones, consisted of embroidery, smocking and quilting. It could all be done with the click of a switch, appearing so easy to the potential customers after a demonstration by trained sales staff.

During this time, Ruth developed a love for sewing. She was eager to learn all she could about dressmaking and her greatest wish was to be able to own the latest machine on the market, the price of which was far beyond her finances. She dreamed as she demonstrated. *One day, maybe - who knows?*

It was while she was employed at the shop in the February of nineteen fifty-two that the news of the King's death was broadcast to the nation. Flags were flown at half-mast in respect; sadness descended on his subjects. He had no son, but his eldest daughter Elizabeth was to take over the throne.

At the time she was in her early twenties, on tour at the Tree Tops Hotel in Kenya with her husband, Phillip. To be The Queen of England - a daunting task for one so young - but one that was expected of her. She returned to London.

Ruth was chosen to dress the shop window to show respect for the late King, and to welcome Elizabeth as the new Queen. Deep purple velvet was chosen for draping round a large photograph of the late King, dressed in ceremonial robes. White lilies were laid on a red velvet cushion along with a bible and crucifix in front of the photograph.

On the other half of the window, laid on dark blue velvet, was a photograph of Elizabeth, smiling across at her father's picture. In front of her, a white cushion held a gold crown and a single red rose.

The effect was simple, but quite nice, the manager told Ruth. She was well pleased at her first attempt at window dressing.

She did not feel very pleased with herself, however, a few months later when the manager summoned her to his office to tell her that she was being dismissed.

"Ruth, you do not put enough pressure on the customers to buy the new machines, and I'm afraid you will never be a good saleswoman. I am very sorry to have to do this, Ruth, as I find you are very courteous and willing, but unfortunately that is not all we want from you as an assistant."

Ruth did not like herself. The disgrace of getting the sack from her first job would, she felt sure, go against her in future attempts to find employment.

Her worries, however, were unfounded, as the manager gave her a very good reference stating that she could do well in some other type of work more suitable for her.

Ruth enrolled at the local labour exchange and awaited their letters to inform her of a vacancy connected to sewing. She did not have long to wait before a letter arrived informing her of an interview at nine thirty the following day at 12 Lord Street. She was up bright and early and dressed in a smart skirt and jumper under her best coat. She left the house with her mum's best wishes for success.

The company she was to attend made specialised children's clothing. The vacancy was for a passer in the sample department.

A warm, friendly woman aged about forty met Ruth at the door and escorted her to a second floor office.

"Sit down here, dear," she said, indicating a chair in front of a large desk. Ruth sat down with a timid smile, her stomach churning.

"I have your reference here, dear. It seems very good, even

though you were dismissed from the job previous. The manager has explained why he thought it necessary to dismiss you. I do understand his motives in doing that, so you need not worry on that account. Now tell me about yourself and what your interests are."

Ruth began by telling her how she liked using the machine and creating garments from pieces of material. She asked politely what type of clothing the company made.

"Come with me, dear, and I will show you round the sewing room so you can see for yourself what we make here." She led the way along a corridor with Ruth close behind her. The building felt warm and friendly, with painted walls in pastel shades. Photographs of small children dotted the walls. As they neared the sewing room, Ruth could hear the buzzing of sewing machines and soft music playing from speakers placed high on the walls. On opening the door to the workroom, the lady revealed a large room with bright lights. Around three dozen women sat happily sewing on long rows of machines, most of them lifting their heads to smile at her as she passed. A door at the end of the room led to a smaller room, equally bright.

Here six women were standing at large tables, surrounded by baskets of clothing. Cardboard boxes of all sizes, along with giant rolls of cellophane, littered the floor.

"This is the sample room, Ruth. Here we pass the garments, checking for mistakes, also cutting off any threads that may have been left on by the sewers. Then we fold up the garments and pack them ready for the reps to take out as samples, hopefully bringing back some orders for us."

Ruth smiled and then shyly asked if she could see some of the samples before they were packed.

"Certainly dear," the lady replied as she walked over to a table. "Janet, can I interrupt you for a moment, please, to show this young lady some of our work?"

The blonde girl working on table two replied,

"Yes of course, Mrs Kent, this batch is lovely. I'm sure she'll like these," she said, as she grinned at Ruth.

From what seemed like a pile of fur fabric, Mrs Kent took out an armful of imitation fur muffs, small pillbox hats with satin ribbons attached and tiny posies of flowers.

"These are to be fastened on the centre of the muffs when Janet has snipped all the bits off, like this, then we pack them all together along with these small matching capes and they're worn over red velvet dresses for weddings."

"They are very pretty" Ruth exclaimed, picturing in her mind tiny tots parading behind lavishly-dressed brides.

"We also make pageboy outfits to match, but we've already packed those, so I can't show you any," Janet told her.

"Another line we do is designer pram rugs. Would you like to see some of them?" Mrs Kent asked.

"Yes please, I would love to," Ruth replied eagerly.

Moving over to another table, Ruth was shown the beautiful soft fluffy pram rugs, some with lambs frolicking among daisies, others with frilly satin ribbons sewn in the shape of a bow at the bottom corner. Many different designs were shown to her, all equally delightful to the eye, in very pale shades of pink, blue or lemon.

Returning to the office, Mrs Kent asked her if she thought she would like a job in the sample department, working with Janet on her table.

"Yes please, Mrs Kent, I would love to work here," Ruth said with absolute delight shining in her eyes.

"Can you start tomorrow at 8.30? We finish at 5 o'clock, with an hour's break for lunch and two ten-minutes breaks for tea twice a day. Your wage will be one pound fifty a week, working Monday to Friday. We keep a week in hand so you will not get any wage for the first week, love, but if you leave at any time this wage will be returned to you. You will also be entitled to one week's holiday the first year, after you have been with us for three months, then the year after you will be entitled to a day for every month you work. Is that all right, dear?"

"Yes. And thank you very much, Mrs Kent for giving me this chance. I'm sure I shall be very happy working here," Ruth answered, with a exceedingly happy heart.

"Mum, where are you?" Ruth shouted, as she dashed excitedly through the door. "I got that job1"

"Well done, love," mum replied entering the room from the kitchen. "I'm so glad for you. Now, tell me all about it."

Ruth was bubbling over with excitement, her face grinning like a Cheshire cat. She told of the beautiful clothing that she had seen and how friendly the staff had been with her.

"I start work tomorrow, I can hardly believe it," she said as she danced from the room, finally taking off her coat which she had forgot about in her excitement.

She awoke bright and early the following morning, full of the joys of spring, skipping like a new lamb around her mum while they prepared for her to leave the house.

"Settle down, lass. You'll need that energy before today is done, no doubt."

Ruth arrived early to take up her place next to Janet on the large sample table.

"Good morning, Ruth," was the cheerful greeting that awaited her as Janet showed her where to stand. "Deary me! You're too small to reach the table properly, lass; I shall have to get you something to stand on," Janet said laughingly, as she went to the corner to fetch a pallet. "This will make you four inches taller, but be careful and remember to step off it before you try to move away."

Ruth thanked her as they began to work together. She found it tiring standing all day, but thoroughly enjoyed the work and hoped she could get used to the standing eventually. The atmosphere was very friendly, the work was clean and the others chatted and laughed about their respective families' escapades. Many jokes were made amidst squeals of laughter, most of which Ruth did not understand.

She remained in this job for two years and liked every minute, until one morning Mrs Kent called everyone into her office for a meeting. She informed them sadly that the firm was moving into larger premises in another town.

"All of you will be guaranteed a job if you are willing to travel each day. Unfortunately we cannot lay transport on due to everyone living in different districts. You have been good staff and I shall be very sorry to lose every one of you. You can have a month to think about it, ladies, as we are not planning on moving for at least six weeks. I would appreciate your decisions at your earliest convenience, please. Believe me when I say I am very sorry to have to give you this bad news. Thank you very much, ladies, that's all I can tell you at this moment."

When Ruth went home that evening, mum knew by her expression that something was wrong.

"What is it, dear?" she enquired, seeing the sad face before her.

"Oh mum," Ruth said with tears pricking her eyes, "the company is moving to another town to larger premises. We can go with them if we want, but it will cost me too much bus fare and it will be too far to travel. I have been so happy there, what am I to do now?"

"Don't worry, love, I'm sure you'll find another job in this town," mum assured her as she took her into her arms to console her. "When do you have to leave?"

"Not for five weeks yet, they've given us time to think it over," Ruth told her tearfully.

"Come on now, let's have your tears dried and we'll have some tea."

During the following month, the women chatted about the move, most of them deciding to go to the new premises. One or two decided it would be impractical for them as they had young children, and it would make it a longer working day with the travelling that would be involved, so they decided to leave along with Ruth.

The dreaded final day arrived at last with mixed emotions, as the women had worked together for a long time and were great friends.

To lose some of their mates was quite sad.

"No work today, ladies, I am taking you all out to lunch," Mrs Kent announced on their arrival. "Come along to my office. Janet, go and make a coffee for us all please. We shall sit there and chat until they come to take the chairs away, then the removal men can get on with the job in peace."

Ruth had spent a very happy two years at the firm, but now it was over she resigned herself to looking for another job.

'Wanted: Machinist for Gentlemen's Tailoring Firm. Experience not necessary as training given,' the advert read.

Ruth applied, and in two weeks was on a machine learning how to tailor gents' suits, also hospital supplies. She gained valuable experience on all types of machines, from straight sewing to buttonhole making; over locking to pressing. The whole spectrum of tailoring was now within her grasp. This time, however, it was piecework. The harder she worked, the more she earned. It was slave labour, rushing all the time to make a decent wage. The workroom was very noisy, lacking the friendliness of her previous job; no one had time to talk. Some jobs were dependent on the previous machinist doing her bit before passing the garment on to the next person for her specific task, before passing it further along the production line. If any machine broke down, it put everyone behind.

Ruth learned, albeit not very easily, to make trousers, waistcoats and jackets. Even strait jackets, which everyone hated doing, thinking of the poor souls who would have to be wearing them. Hospital supplies consisted of sheets, pillowcases and surgeon's aprons and gowns. These were good for wage-making, as the work involved was quick but exceedingly boring.

As she was growing up, she made friends. Most of them paid their own board, allowing them to have more money for themselves to buy the latest clothes, a young girl's priority. Boys were the main topic of conversation, along with what to wear for the latest date.

Just out of the town, a firm made electric motors at a large factory that paid very good wages. Ruth applied for a job there and got one winding starter motors. The work was so different to what she had done before. Sometimes it was heavy swinging the larger motors round in the cradles as the wires were wound in to a set pattern. Other times it was very fiddly on the tiny motors that were hardly big enough to get her fingers between, forcing the wires into minute grooves. Sore fingers were an occupational hazard every day. Washing hands that had been caught by the motors and cut with the wires was at times a very painful operation.

Small thimbles were made every day out of plaster on a regular basis before commencing work. These offered some protection, but soon became tatty as they also got cut to shreds and needed replacing. The wages, however, compensated for the hazards of the job: Ruth made three times the wages she had earned before.

She made many friends of her own age, including one very special one whose name was Mary. A firm friendship developed between them. Mary had been born in Scotland, but following her parents' divorce she had moved to Yorkshire along with her mother. Ruth found it difficult to understand what she was talking about at first, but soon learnt some of the Scottish expressions Mary used, enabling her to understand her better. They were the same height, but Mary was a little fatter. She had very dark hair and eyes to match. The two of them were the same age, yet Mary seemed older than Ruth - maybe because she was more worldly-wise. She was also very good-looking, unlike Ruth, who was quite plain. They were inseparable, both with the same quiet temperament and sharing the same interests in films and books. Each day they laughed together as they shared sandwiches at lunch time, the other one's always tasting nicer than their own.

During the evenings they went together to the local cinema or dancehall, sometimes staying at each other's homes to chat and compare clothes bought on a visit to the local shopping centre the previous weekend.

Mary was more of a sister to Ruth than Elizabeth, who had turned into quite a tomboy, having completely different interests to Ruth.

Mary had had a troubled life due to her parents being divorced and remarried. Both of her parents bitterly resented each other, so whenever they met up Mary was usually in the middle of the trouble.

Ruth had met Mary's father, who lived in Scotland, many times but on his visits he was usually drunk and swore like a trooper. Every second word was something she was not used to, unless Mr Briggs was very angry, and the Scottish accent somehow made it sound much worse than it was. She could sense Mary's shame each time it happened.

Her mother was loud-mouthed and blunt, always getting onto Mary about something or other. *Little wonder Mary is quiet,* thought Ruth on many occasions. It must have been difficult for her to get a word in edgeways between them when they had all lived together.

Mary lived in a large Victorian house which had been converted into flats. It had a large window overlooking the main road. The room was gigantic and the kitchen small, but it had a fridge and cooker for her own use. The bathroom, however, was communal so having a bath was by appointment only. This was not very easy, as some tenants took advantage if the door was open. Luckily, the toilet was separate.

There was ample furniture in Mary's room: two fireside chairs, a table and two chairs for eating, plus a large, old-fashioned iron bedstead complete with feather mattress. Ruth loved to stay the night after a visit to the cinema or a late dance, the two of them curling up together after coming in from the cold and sinking into the feathers - absolute bliss. The following morning they set off for work together after a breakfast made by Mary in her little kitchen, laughing along the way about something that had happened the previous evening.

Mary soon found herself a boyfriend, so Ruth's visits became less frequent. Albert was a tall, skinny man with quiet ways. He was much older than Mary. His hair was darker than Mary's and he was quite tall, towering over Mary, who was only just over five feet tall. Albert was quite ordinary-looking - nothing spectacular at all - but with quiet ways. Mary was pretty, with a dimple in her chin and an elfin face, whereas Ruth was skinny and plain with big teeth and a long, thin face, weighing seven stone wet through. Ruth had always envied Mary's looks, but it did not interfere with their friendship at all. Albert, however, had a smile that melted Mary's heart ever time she saw him. She idolised him from the very beginning.

"You must come out with us just the same," she told Ruth. "Albert doesn't mind one little bit if we go as a threesome. You're always welcome at our house."

Ruth, however, felt she was intruding, so declined Mary's invitations.

It was not many months before Mary told Ruth that Albert had proposed to her and they were to be married.

They married on a quiet Saturday afternoon at the local register office. It was a quiet ceremony with Ruth and a cousin of Mary's as witnesses. There was to be no honeymoon, but the four of them went for a meal at a highly recommended restaurant, after which Mary and Albert went home together with very best wishes for a happy life together.

Not long after this, during a visit to the local cinema with Elizabeth, Ruth noticed a young man watching them during the interval. The girls giggled together, wondering which of the two he was watching. On leaving, he approached them and turned to Ruth, asking her if she would like to go out on a date with him.

He was tall with fair hair and blue eyes, rather slim and very smart in an army uniform. Ruth liked the look of him and decided that, yes, she would go out with him.

The following evening they met outside the cinema.

"Shall we go to the cafe for a glass of Coke and get to know each other a little?" he asked. Ruth agreed and together they walked the short distance to the café, where most of the young people gathered to listen to the latest pop records on the jukebox.

Sitting at a table, he told her his name was Harry. He was eighteen years old and had just done his basic training for the national service. He had a younger brother called Steven and two sisters. One was older and the other one younger than him. His brother was not a well boy due to heart trouble, and had needed constant care since childhood. Harry appeared to think a great deal about his brother, and as he talked Ruth could sense the worry in him. Harry's family lived about a mile away from Ruth's. He was stationed away in the next town, but was able to get home quite often in the evenings. Ruth told him about her sister and her friend Mary who had just got married, and about where she worked. Though she felt quite shy talking about herself, she decided she could get on with Harry very well eventually as she liked his company.

"Where would you like to go?" he asked her. "Shall we go for a walk?" The park was not very far away, so together they strolled, chatting about various things. The evening was pleasant, with the birds singing before taking up their resting places for the night.

Other couples were in the park, strolling hand-in-hand, looking for quiet places for a quick kiss or cuddle. The scent of roses wafted through the air from the archway as they passed. Beautiful blooms of deep burgundy mixed with pink, entwined over the trellis mingling with Jasmine and creating a heavenly scent. Bees were humming around the blossoms, collecting honey to take back to the hives further along the park paths.

A few men were playing bowls and they stopped for a while to watch, not really understanding the rules of the game. Around the corner, birds were chattering in the aviary; budgerigars and canaries, along with a few parrots squabbling amongst themselves.

They stopped and watched their antics, laughing together along with a number of other couples, after which they decided to go back to the café for a cup of coffee, as the evening had turned a little chilly.

After a little chat they walked home, Harry leaving Ruth at her street end and giving her a quick peck on the cheek as he left. He promised to meet her four days later at the same spot outside the cinema.

She arrived early for the date, but after half an hour Harry had not appeared, so Ruth went home alone. *Well, that's it,* she thought. *No romance.*

The following week, however, she bumped into Harry as he was coming away from the railway station. He apologised for not turning up at the date, explaining that he had not known how to get in touch with her because he did not know her address or phone number. He had stayed at the camp on extra duties due to the volatile situation in the Middle East at the time.

She forgave him and the romance continued.

It was late autumn 1956 when trouble was looming in the Middle East. General Gamel Abdul Nasser started a revolution and formed a military coup, ousting King Farouk. He claimed the Suez Canal as Egyptian property and threatened Israel. The combined monies of the French and English had built the Canal. At the same time, Arch-Bishop Makarios and General Grivas were in conflict over Cyprus and troops were put on standby.

Harry was told to report for duty at short notice, barely giving him chance to think about anything, and within days he was packed and on his way to the station along with other young men from his group. He bid Ruth farewell on the station platform, not knowing really where they were going apart from somewhere in the Malta region.

The train pulled away with Ruth not knowing when she would see Harry again. She stood waving until the train was out of sight before the tears began to run down her face.

It was quite a while before a letter arrived for her at last from Harry with a Cyprus postmark.

The EOKA terrorists were very busy at the time in the Troudos mountain area of Cyprus, according to the news bulletins Ruth had heard on the radio. Harry was there, and she became very troubled.

Harry kept writing and his letters were cheerful. He seemed to be enjoying it, but still she worried, especially when she heard reports of people being hurt.

Mary and Albert kept her company and she visited Harry's parents on a number of occasions, so time passed quickly.

Mary arrived at work one morning with good news for Ruth.

"We're going to have a baby!" she told Ruth, with the excitement clearly showing in her face.

Ruth told her she was delighted at the news.

"Now I can pass my time knitting and sewing for the new arrival. I have plenty of time on my hands now, with Harry being away."

Mary had a trouble-free pregnancy and her son arrived on time in April the following year. He was a fine, healthy lad and they all adored him. He had inherited Mary's dimpled chin and elfin face, and his hair was dark and spiky, giving him a cute pixie look.

Mary knew from the start that she would have no trouble getting a babysitter, as Ruth was enchanted with their son and very willing and able to oblige at any time.

DISCOVERIES

It was while Harry was away that Ruth changed her job once more. This time she wanted to dress a little smarter for work instead of wearing overalls all the time. A job opportunity arose as a cashier and ledger clerk at the local furniture store, so she applied, was accepted and began work the following week. The work was easy and much more interesting, as she met the public and many a cheerful word passed between them.

On entering the office one morning, a new girl working there spoke to Ruth.

"I know you from the orphanage, Ruth. My adopted brother came from there and I remember you. Your father got married shortly before you and your sister left."

Ruth stood dumbfounded at her remarks.

"What are you saying?" she asked.

"I remember the wedding, because my mum and I were passing the registry office as they were coming out. We thought you'd be going home not long after that, and you did."

An extremely puzzled Ruth went home that night.

"Mum, a girl who's just started at work has told me today that she remembered your wedding to dad. Tell me she's wrong - she can't be right about that, can she?"

The look of shock on the face of Alice was enough to tell Ruth that the news was correct.

"When was it, mum?"

She got no answer, just an outburst of tears and no further mention of the subject.

The news shocked Ruth to the core. Alice was not her mum, so who was? Shadows of the past began to loom. Alice refused to discuss anything and Ruth dare not approach her father. The only answer was for her to find out for herself.

Ruth pondered the situation over in her mind for a few days

before coming to the conclusion that she would have to do some serious research into the matter of clues as to her identity. Deciding that the phone book was a valuable source of information, she began to search for her surname in the town where she was born. The results were not too good, but it did yield a few. By means of phone calls, she was able to eliminate a lot of possibilities.

One contact gave her other phone numbers of people that could maybe help her in her search. She eventually succeeded in her efforts, and traced a man whose father had the same name as hers. He had lost contact through some sort of family dispute in his younger years but said he would be interested in meeting her. An arrangement was made between them for Ruth to visit him at his home the following weekend. Not wishing to upset mum any further, she said nothing of the intended visit, so her mum thought that she was visiting Mary as usual.

She was welcomed, but not too warmly, by a man who had a lovely wife and five daughters with him when he greeted her at the door to their home.

His name was Gordon. He was sixteen years older than her and told her he had a sister that was older still but did not know where she lived at that time, as she had recently divorced and they had lost contact for the time being. He and his family were in the process of emigrating to New Zealand and were waiting for confirmation that everything was all right for the job he expecting to take up when he got there.

He looked just like her father, and they discovered in the course of conversation that indeed they shared the same father, but a different mother due to her father's deserting his mother when he was a young boy. He had no kind words to say about his father, so she presumed that it had been a rather bitter time for all concerned.

He had not heard anything about his father since childhood, but had not been concerned about what had happened to him.

Ruth visited Gordon on many occasions and really got to know the family well. She liked him, despite his rather adverse welcome to her, and felt regret at not knowing about him in her early years. Even with Gordon's obvious reluctance to make her a friend, his family always made her very welcome each time that she visited them.

She knew she would have to approach her father and pluck up the courage to tell him that she knew about their existence if she was to find out what the true story was about her mother. She felt rather afraid of her father's reaction to the news that she knew about Gordon, but never did she imagine for one moment how bad would be the reaction from her father, or how badly he would take it.

"You have no right to pry into my past!" he yelled at her. "I have always looked after you well," he continued, with what to Ruth seemed a look of hatred in his eyes.

Alice by now was in floods of tears.

"How could you, Ruth? Why did you find it necessary to open up old wounds for your father?" she sobbed.

"Please mum, forgive me," she begged. "I had to know, but you wouldn't say anything about it."

"Well, now you know," yelled her father. "You can go and live your precious Gordon as from tomorrow!"

Ruth stared at him, thinking he could not mean this.

But mean it he did.

NEW BEGINNINGS

With her father's angry words, another chapter in Ruth's book of life was about to begin.

The following morning, a fellow workman noticed Ruth's tearstained face.

"Whatever is the problem, lass?" he asked.

His words opened a floodgate of tears as Ruth told him about the situation at home. She tried to explain fully the story of what she had done to enrage her father so very much.

"Well, don't you worry, lass. We have a spare room at our house and I'm sure the missus would love to have some company for our little lassie. She's only five, and gets quite fed up playing by herself. She wears me and my missus out. We'll go and see her at lunchtime, shall we?"

Ruth arranged with William and his wife to rent the spare room for a month's trial so that if her father had a change of heart she could go back home.

A tearful Alice met Ruth on her return home.

"I don't agree with your father, love, but I have to abide by his decision whether I like it or not, or I'll be in trouble as well. I'm so sorry, Ruth, but there's nothing I can do to change his mind."

Ruth put her arms around the only woman she had known as a mother.

"Don't worry, mum, I've found somewhere to stay with a family and I think it will be alright there. I shall keep in touch with you when dad's not at home."

"Just give him time to cool off and maybe he'll have a change of heart, dear," Alice replied with a hug.

Together they packed Ruth's meagre belongings and bade each other a tearful farewell for the time being. Ruth climbed into the taxi for another new beginning.

During the first week in her new home, Ruth wrote to Harry

telling him of her new address and the events that had taken place to cause it. She continued to visit her half brother and his family, also telling him about her father's reaction to the news that she had managed to trace him and the anger he had shown.

The suggestion came up that maybe, under the circumstances, she might like to consider going with them to New Zealand as part of the family. Gordon hesitantly said he would make enquiries while Ruth had a chance to think it over. *Why not?* she asked herself, *there's nothing to keep me here now, except Harry. My father has disowned me, so it will be very difficult to keep in touch with mum and will only cause her more anguish every time I call; maybe I could be happy with Gordon and his girls. They seem to like me. I could get a job there and be self-supporting, and not be a burden to them.*

Once more Ruth put pen to paper, this time to tell Harry of the possibility of her going to New Zealand with her half-brother and his family.

It was not long before she received an answer from Harry begging her not to be hasty.

"Please don't go, Ruth," he pleaded. *"It's my intention to get engaged when I come home on leave the next time."*

As the weeks progressed, Ruth was more and more undecided. She knew that if she was going to New Zealand, she would have to depart before Harry could get any leave, therefore she would never see him again. The decision was very hard to make. A new life with a family she had not known before all this, or stay in her own country and marry Harry.

Gordon was her half-brother, but they did not have the same mother and that was the thing that helped to sway Ruth in her decision.

The story of her life so far was very incomplete.

After talking it through once more with Gordon and spending lots of sleepless nights tossing the pros and cons over in her mind, pondering the best thing to do, she sensed his reluctance and made her decision to stay.

She loved Harry, and maybe it was possible that she would not settle in a strange country. Once there, she would find it very difficult to return to her homeland alone without the help of Gordon.

The departure date came at last, after all the frantic packing had been completed. The parties were over; there were just sad farewells to be made.

"Please don't write to me," she asked Gordon. "I don't want to know how it is over there or I might regret my decision. Thank you for your friendship these last few months and I wish you and the family well in your new life. My one regret is that I've grown up not knowing you." Ruth hugged each one in turn and bade them bon voyage with a sad heart.

Once more the tears fell as she quietly closed the door and walked away, knowing that she would never see them again.

HOMECOMING

Harry's stay in that glorious, sun-soaked island of Cyprus was to last for thirteen months. At last the day dawned that he was coming home. Ruth was high in the clouds all day, unable to concentrate on anything other than his return.

The clock crept agonisingly slowly round to the hour of his arrival, and each time the phone rang her heart missed a beat.

The time to go home arrived, but there was no Harry, nor any word from him. The appointed hour had passed without any sight or sound of him.

Ruth felt great disappointment as she walked to the bus stop to go home. Perhaps he had not really meant what he had said in his letters, she thought. Her heart was heavy. However, her disappointment vanished like a wisp of smoke in a gentle breeze as soon as she opened the door to her home. Ruth fell in love with him all over again as she rushed into his arms.

"Oh, how I've missed you! It's so good to see you," she bubbled with delight.

Harry stood before her, his sun-kissed body a golden brown, his hair almost white, his eyes bluer than the ocean he had left behind on a faraway shore. He seemed much more grown up than she remembered and more self-assured. Ruth felt she could melt in his arms as he caressed her lovingly.

"It's so nice to be home again. I've missed you also, Ruth," he said gently as he enfolded her in his arms.

For the following days, Ruth was in seventh heaven, blissfully happy. They spent as much time together as was possible, some of it with his fellow soldier pals and their girlfriends, other times at his or her house. She spent the weekends at Harry's home, where she was treated like one of the family.

One such time they were alone in the house, and when their kisses became more ardent and passionate Ruth gave herself to Harry in a moment of tender abandonment.

As the months passed, Ruth realised the consequences of their actions: she was pregnant. Harry was not unduly concerned when she told him the news; neither were his parents. They were told that they were sensible enough to have the responsibility of a child and had known each other quite a long time, so what was the problem?

The trouble, as far as Ruth was concerned, was where they were going to live.

As the tiny speck of humanity grew inside her, Ruth knew that they could not leave it much longer before they found a place to live and make into a home for their impending family.

Together they toured the housing agencies without any success, disappointed each time they thought they had found a place which turned out to be unsuitable each time due to too many steps to the entrance, or nowhere to put a pram, or to being much too expensive.

The council would not give them a house until the child was born. They tried the private landlords again, but again were disappointed in the homes that were on offer. Some were no better than hovels: how anyone was expected to live in them was beyond Ruth's comprehension. The others that were in a reasonable state were far too expensive for them. Harry and his family spent as much time as they could searching for a suitable place for them.

Finally, in desperation, Ruth called at the local Citizens Advice Bureau. She was presented to a woman looking anything but friendly and was asked in a rather brusque manner, "What is the problem, madam?"

Ruth informed her of her plight and asked if she could help. Slowly the woman got to her feet and left the room, saying she would not be long. She reappeared with an address.

"The gentleman who lives at this address has a room to let," she informed Ruth. "I will phone him to say you are coming to have a look at it, shall I?"

"Yes, please," Ruth replied, and fixed a time when Harry would be able to go with her.

They arrived at the house, which was semi-detached with a large bay window to the front. It looked quite nice, so Ruth felt a little better about the situation.

"Harry, it will do for the time being 'until we can find somewhere of our own," she said hopefully. "If it's all right inside. It has a garden for me to put the baby out in its pram in the fresh air. It's in a nice area, and it should be quite peaceful here among the trees."

Harry nodded in agreement with a smile.

"Let's hope he doesn't want too much rent for it. We won't want too much furniture for it for a start, and then maybe we can save for something better very quickly. I shall be demobbed soon, so I will have to get a job pretty quickly because you won't be able to work for very long."

He took hold of Ruth's hand and together they approached the door and rang the bell. It seemed to take ages before the door was opened by a large, friendly-faced man holding two walking sticks. His face was ruddy, his hair greying at the temples and worry lines were etched across his forehead around his eyes and mouth.

As he leaned against the wall, he stretched his hand out to Harry.

"Come in, lad," he said in a strong foreign accent as he awkwardly opened the door to allow them to pass.

"You will have to be patient with me as I find it rather difficult to walk today," he said as he turned to face them. "What I can offer you is a double bedroom to yourselves, but you will have to share the kitchen and bathroom with my other lodger and me. He has his own bedroom, like me, but we need to come into the kitchen to do our cooking. You can use it for the rest of the time to yourselves, as it has a nice coal fire in there. The other lodger is a teacher and travels home each weekend, so he is only here in the evenings during the week when we both use the lounge together."

Very slowly he led the way around the house, which appeared clean but very untidy until they reached the bedroom he was offering them. This room was completely empty.

"You will of course have to furnish it yourself," he informed them, as they had expected.

The bathroom was presentable and adequate for their needs.

As he led the way through into the kitchen, Ruth noticed that the cooker appeared very modern and the fridge standing alongside it looked to be recently purchased.

Across the room stood two comfortable-looking armchairs placed in front of a warm coal fire. Towards the centre of the room stood a card table and two hard-backed chairs supplied for eating purposes.

"The rent will be thirteen pounds a week, payable on the Friday," he told Harry. "Let me know by the end of the week if you are interested, please." Harry and Ruth shook hands with him and left to think it over.

Their baby was due in three months' time, so the situation was getting quite desperate.

"I think we should accept it, don't you?" Harry enquired of Ruth as they walked out of the garden gate. "The area is nice. I know it's not going to be very easy with a new baby and two men around the house besides me, but hopefully it will only be a temporary measure. It's not too bad for a start and it means we can get married as soon as possible."

They both agreed, and decided to go and start making arrangements for their wedding the next day.

Ruth visited Alice and told her the news. She was shocked at first, but accepted it.

"You know your father won't come to the wedding, don't you dear?" she said sadly. But it was only as Ruth had expected, so she was not surprised by her mother's remark.

"You will come, won't you, mum?"

"Well dear, I don't see that I can, due to your father's being home on Saturdays. I shan't be able to get out without him knowing, will I?"

"Oh mum, I shall miss you, but it will only be a very quiet affair with just two witnesses. We shall be getting married at the registry office by special licence to save time, as we want to get moved in as soon a possible. It's a good thing I don't need my father's consent or then I might have had a problem, don't you think?"

Together they had a little laugh at this remark.

"Well, I wish you all the best in your future life with Harry, my dear. Have a happy life, Ruth, with your hubby and child. I shall think about you on your wedding day and say a prayer for your happiness together, love." Mum gave Ruth a hug and Ruth knew that her mother's heart was sad.

The wedding was arranged for the Whitsuntide weekend. The sun was shining as Ruth dressed in her pale blue suit, attaching a small spray of freesia to her jacket. The birds were singing and all was right in her world once more. She knew her father would not be attending, so she had arranged for William to give her away in his place. Harry's family was going to be there, as well as William's wife and daughter.

There was no taxi with white ribbons streaming from the bonnet waiting for her as she stepped out of the door. She made her way to the local bus stop with her adopted family, thinking that this was not quite what she had dreamed of as a young girl for her wedding day.

Harry was standing waiting for her when she arrived at the registry office. Arm in arm, they went in together after a quick cuddle.

The registrar was just about to speak when the door flew open and in came her mother, followed closely behind by her father.

Ruth's happiness was complete as she said her vows, whispering to herself a silent prayer of thanks.

After the ceremony, her father insisted that they all went together for a meal as a treat from him and asked her to forgive a stupid old man for his rather foolish behaviour. During the meal he told her he had gone into work that morning for a rush job but had been so troubled by his conscience that he had had to leave and attend his daughter's wedding to give her his blessing for a happy life.

Ruth was happy - she was married to Harry, she was friends against with her father and her family was reunited. What a joyous day it had turned out to be after all!

Part II

THE LANDLORD

The new landlord was a disabled miner. He was allocated a coal allowance each month and this was tipped unceremoniously onto the roadside each time in one large heap. It was obvious to Ruth that he could do nothing about this and she wondered how he had managed to get it all into the house before. She also knew that there was nothing she could do to help in her present state, as she had great difficulty seeing her own feet, never mind carrying coal into the bunker. Poor Harry would have to do it when he came home from work. This happened every month. Sometimes the teacher was around to help, but mostly it fell to Harry. He did not mind, as it kept his wife and child warm.

The living conditions were far from ideal, as Ruth found to her dismay as soon as she had to give up work and spend the full day around the house. The landlord wanted to spend his time with them when the schoolmaster was away at the weekend, so they never seemed to be alone except in their bedroom. The crippling illness the landlord suffered was multiple sclerosis, which meant that some days he was fine, but other days he would not be well and found it very difficult to keep his balance, sometimes falling in the most awkward of places. Being confined to the house, he was a desperately lonely man in need of constant company.

Ruth was sure he did not invade their privacy on purpose, but when he came into the kitchen to make a cup of tea he would stay on and on, drinking his tea while sitting at their table, lingering as long as he could but not talking about anything in particular.

They both felt extremely sorry for him, as he was a nice man and watching him struggling to keep his balance was very sad. He was a proud man, so didn't want them to help him unless it was absolutely necessary, such as when he fell over.

Ruth's heart went out to him many a time as she watched him fight to obtain stability while shaking from head to toe on his walking sticks. He was also very religious and would talk to her many times about his dearest wish to go to Lourdes. He had convinced himself that if he could get there, he would be cured; his faith was that strong. He had photographs of the shrine all over the lounge. He knew that a bus called 'Across' had taken many people to Lourdes and was staffed by volunteers to assist the invalids during their journey and when they got there.

Much as Ruth felt sorry for him, he also aggravated her. His favourite meal appeared to be fried beans and bacon, and Ruth was constantly cleaning the cooker after his frying attempts, which left fat splashes everywhere.

Another problem was his socks: when they had developed a hole, they were thrown under the kitchen sink, sometimes unwashed, so that eventually they began to smell a little ripe. Ruth discovered a huge pile one day after she had seen him shutting the cupboard door. Each one had a hole, so she set herself to darning. When the sewing was finished, she filled the kitchen sink with hot water and soapsuds, leaving them to soak for an hour and then washing the lot. There were blues, greens, reds, greys, blacks - every colour under the rainbow blowing on the line in the breeze. She tried to imagine what the neighbours would think as they saw them, and had to laugh.

Harry began to tidy the garden up, which was quite large but very overgrown with weeds.

"We can grow our own vegetables; that will help the housekeeping out a bit. It's a shame to waste all this good growing space on weeds."

"Yes, Harry," Ruth smiled. "I'll get some plants next time I go to the shops. What sort shall I get?"

"How about getting some cabbages, cauliflower, sprouts - or anything else they have? I don't know when the seasons are for planting such things, really. I'm sure we shall be able to eat them all between us - you know, they'll be good for you in your state of health," Harry laughed as he gave her a squeeze. "I won't be able to get my arms around you soon," he said as he rubbed her protruding stomach.

The day finally arrived for the landlord to go on his dream journey to Lourdes. The trip had been arranged for him through his local church after a few visits from the priest. He was so happy as he prepared his things with the help of Ruth, and eagerly awaited the taxi that was to take him to the coach in the town centre and his escort for the next few days. His faith was so strong that his excitement was catching as Ruth helped him into the waiting car.

As he left, she prayed that his faith would be rewarded with a cure and that indeed a miracle would happen for him to give him back his health.

Sadly, however, this was not to be. He returned a mere shadow of the man who had left three weeks earlier, full of hope. The journey had been too much for him, travelling day and night on the coach both there and back. He looked totally dejected and his eyes no longer held the glow of hope with which he had left his home. He was shaking more than before he had gone: the miracle they had both prayed for had not happened.

Ruth cried inside for him, for now he had nothing but despair to look forward to and the knowledge that his health would get worse as time progressed. His life was destined to become a never-ending trial of endurance.

FIRSTBORN

As the time grew near for Ruth to give birth to their first child, her father seemed unduly worried. She did not know at that time of the circumstances of her sister's birth. Her slim body resembled a beach ball and excitement grew along with it day by day as the delivery date approached. She was impatient to be a mother.

Unfortunately, the date passed by without even a twinge, much to her disappointment.

"Nine months is long enough without going longer," she groaned to Harry as they climbed into bed that night, both equally disappointed that their child was not making an appearance that day.

On her next visit to the antenatal clinic, Ruth was happy to hear that she had to report in the next day to be admitted. Once there, they were to induce labour for her as she was quite large enough and in their opinion the baby had reached full term.

As she packed her case the following morning she felt a little apprehensive, not knowing what was involved in inducing labour. She discovered later that it was nothing to be afraid of, as it took a matter of minutes to break her waters and within the hour she was in labour.

The child was born eight hours later and the birth was not too difficult. As she held the infant girl in her arms for the first time, she shed tears of joy.

"She's mine, all mine," she whispered to herself, wanting to sing it out loud for the whole world to hear.

She said a silent prayer of thanks as she stared in disbelief at the tiny child that lay cradled in her arms, a masterpiece of perfection from the tiny nose to the ten little toes. he tiny babe, weighing six and a half pounds, was here at last.

Ruth marvelled at the perfect angelic face; the blonde, fluffy hair standing up like down on the tiny head; the minute nails, pink and perfect on her fingers and toes.

As the child cried for the first time Ruth thought that this surely was the greatest miracle of all time.

Harry beamed when he saw the baby and tenderly picked her up, looking at Ruth with tears in his eyes.

"She's gorgeous, Ruth. What are we calling her?"

"What about Beverly Anne?" she replied.

"Yes, that's a nice name." And so it was.

The pains of childbirth were soon forgotten as the three of them sat so happily together, smiling like Cheshire cats. For her departure from hospital, Ruth dressed Beverly Anne in a tiny white dress trimmed with rose buds, a cardigan, bootees and a bonnet trimmed with swansdown. To complete the outfit was a tiny cape provided by Alice.

Harry met them at the door and gently escorted Ruth down the steps to the waiting taxi with the child in her arms.

They soon settled in to the new routine. Beverly was breast-fed by Ruth, so there were no problems with having to mix feeds during the night, and as time progressed Beverly grew into a happy, contented baby.

Ruth enjoyed her new role as mother and was blissfully happy. Stars shone from her eyes and her heart was brimming over with happiness; her life was full of joy and contentment, which was something that had eluded her until now.

The landlord, however, was not quite as thrilled with the new baby in the house.

The winter was fast approaching, bringing colder weather with it and meaning that the electric bills were now going to be higher. The coal was not going to last as long, as the fire was lit much earlier every day.

He asked for more rent from Ruth and Harry, but they were just coping as it was, for Harry did not get a large wage. Paying out more in rent would be difficult, if not almost impossible.

"I think we should try and find somewhere else," Harry told Ruth with regret.

She agreed with him, so once more they were house-hunting, but this time with better results and more success.

A small house was available, 'two up, one down,' as the agent put it.

"No bathroom, but it has a very large sitting room with a kitchen area in it and a very large cellar."

"We're interested in looking at it, please," they told him and he handed them the key.

Together Ruth and Harry viewed the property that was situated on a busy bypass road but stood well back from the kerb. There was no garden this time, and Harry remembered all his hard work on the other garden that now would be wasted if they moved.

The teacher would eat his vegetables, and that thought disappointed him as he had not had any help whatsoever from the teacher in the early days when all the hard digging had been done.

On entering the house they were pleasantly surprised: the small vestibule opened into a huge room. In one corner a recess held a deep, white pot sink in nice, clean, modern-looking cupboards, complete with water heating on the wall, to the right of which was a cooker point.

A tiled fireplace stood to the left of the cupboards and this also was in good condition. Ruth pictured a nice coal fire burning brightly in the grate as she followed Harry down the stairs to the cellar.

Whitewashed walls greeted them, immaculately clean; also a large stone shelf and a wooden cupboard with a wire mesh front to keep the food free from flies. Leaving the cellar, they climbed together up the stairs to the bedrooms.

These also were exceptionally clean. One of them was quite small, but large enough to make a nursery. The master bedroom was just as large as the lounge down below.

"Goodness, Harry, we shall need loads of furniture to furnish this house," Ruth said in dismay.

"I agree with you, love, but we shall just have to get a little at a time when we can afford it, and we won't be paying all that rent. We'll get the essentials first, and at least we can call it home and ours

- not sharing with others like we have been. It will be so grand to have a house to ourselves for a change," he said cheerfully as he took her into his arms and gave her a hug. "We'll manage. I shall have to work overtime a bit more 'until we can get on our feet, that's all. Don't worry."

Harry kept his word and soon the carpet arrived, to be followed by the table and chairs. The room was so large that the carpet only fitted in the centre, leaving a large area around showing the stone flags.

"I have an idea! Ruth, we can get some roofing felt very cheaply and cover the rest of the floor for the time being, and we can paint it to match the carpet as we'll never be able to buy a carpet big enough for this room. If we paint it, it will look like linoleum," he told her, but Ruth could not quite picture it.

The following day Harry brought the felt and together they laid it with a bit of a struggle. He had also bought a tin of red Dulux paint, which he proceeded to paint onto the felt. The end result was quite remarkable and it gave the room a very warm appearance; both of them were well pleased with the result.

The house was at last beginning to look homely when Alice told them that a neighbour had died and the house needed emptying.

"There's a lot of furniture; rather old fashioned but very sturdy. You must come and have a look at it yourselves to see if there's anything you'd like. It's going very cheap to get rid of it, and it's no good me looking at it for you."

"Yes, mum, we'd love to see it," both agreed together. "That might be the answer to our prayers. We'll come after Harry has finished work tomorrow."

"Don't worry about that. They're not in need of the money - they just need to get the house emptied – I'm sure we can come to some arrangement about it, as they do realise how you're fixed."

"I'll see you tomorrow, then" Ruth called as she left to go home.

The following evening it was like entering a treasure trove for Ruth and Harry. Beautiful mahogany furniture met their gaze, all polished with loving care over many years. Pots, pans, bedding, - everything they could possibly need was available to them.

"You can have the lot for fifty pounds," the vendor told their unbelieving ears. "If I sell it to anyone else the price will go up a lot more. You will care for it, I'm sure, and that would please my old aunt as she loved her furniture all these past years. I'm sure she would approve of you taking it. If you want it, you can pay me ten quid a week starting at the end of the month; that gives you three weeks to arrange for it to be moved."

Ruth and Harry could not believe what they were hearing.

"That's all right, isn't it Harry?" asked Ruth.

"It sure is," he replied with a grin spreading from ear to ear, absolutely amazed at the offer.

LIFE AT NUMBER 12: CHRISTMAS 1958

Ruth opened the door of number twelve to the furniture deliverymen and the precious mahogany furniture was carefully carried in. She fussed around until she got it in the right place to show it off to its best advantage, almost making Harry dizzy with her excitement. The poor soul was exhausted by the time it was finally settled into the correct place for her. Harry slowly sank into one of the armchairs with a glint of humour in his eyes.

"It's beautiful, Harry; it looks so nice. We are lucky, don't you think?" Ruth said as she crept onto his tired knee. "Now our home is really complete. I'm so happy, I could burst."

"It will soon be Christmas," Harry replied. "I hope you won't be expecting a present after all this," he said with a laugh, giving Ruth a playful nip.

"No, Harry," was her reply as she wrapped her arms round him, squeezing him tightly. "Harry, I have everything I could possibly want in the world here with you and our baby."

From the bottom of her heart she meant it.

After settling into their new home, Ruth made arrangements for Beverly to be baptised at the local Church. Her sister Elizabeth and her friend Mary were chosen to be godmothers. Ruth had bought a beautiful long Swiss lace dress for her child to wear, together with a bonnet and matching bootees, trimmed with the swansdown like she used to make.

Beverly looked absolutely gorgeous as Harry proudly took photographs of her, and Ruth felt the teardrops of happiness enter her eyes. She felt so very proud as she handed her baby to Elizabeth in the church to be baptised in the Church of England faith as the babe looked up into the vicar's eyes in wonderment.

Next door to number twelve lived a frail old lady called Jessie, who had lived alone for a number of years following the death of her husband. Jessie wasted very little time in introducing herself to them. The highlight of her day was to call round at number twelve 'to see the baby,' this being her excuse, but Ruth knew she was lonely. And did not mind, as she rather liked the old lady and always made her welcome, even if it was a little inconvenient at the time.

Beverly's eyes would light up when she heard Jessie's croaky little voice.

"And how's my little pal today, then?" she would ask.

Number twelve was a back-to-back house. Amy, who was Jessie's friend, lived in the one behind Ruth and Harry. She was not as inquisitive as Jessie and did not call unless she was going to the shop, which was every other day.

Ruth always put the kettle on and asked the two old ladies to sit and have a cup of tea with her and a chat, which they were both extremely willing to do. They both knew all the local gossip, which was passed on to Ruth daily without her asking.

Babies were a rare sight in the neighbourhood, and each time Ruth ventured out with her child they all made quite a fuss of her. Shopping took twice as long with all the chattering, and Ruth sometimes wished she could just dash out and back again without being seen.

Jessie had a habit of taking two aspirin tablets each morning and a pinch of snuff several times a day. She never seemed to ail anything, not even a cold in the winter. Her house was spotless, although a little threadbare and lonely-looking. It was too tidy; not even a pair of slippers littered the floor. Ruth never minded her dropping in, as she knew that she must be terribly lonely living alone, but it was always so hard to get away from her.

Jessie and Amy got so much pleasure from being with Beverley that Ruth found it brought her happiness too, seeing the smiles on their faces each time they talked to the baby. She was happy that she could bring a little sunshine into what must have been two very miserable lives before Harry, herself and their bright-eyed smiling bundle of mischief had moved into their neighbourhood.

The weather was rapidly changing, the darkness coming in very early and the cold winds beginning to bite. Everyone was very busy preparing for Christmas. The shops in the town were ablaze with colour and decorations all over. The streets were twinkling with fairy lights and carols played everywhere for all to hear.

Ruth wanted it to be a lovely time for her family; their first together with Beverley in their own home. She wanted to make it so special. With Harry, she bought her first tree and fairy lights, trimmings for the walls, a small nativity scene for the sideboard and candles for the table, along with some holly and tinsel. The following day Ruth began to shop for the food and presents they would need.

Harry had secretly saved some money for her to spend, which he gave her as she prepared Beverly for the cold weather. Together, they set off for the town.

On her arrival at the market, Ruth put her purse into her pocket to enable her to take Beverly out of her pram. She could not leave her alone outside a shop; she was far too precious. Ruth went into the shop and browsed through the goods on display, then selected a number of items for presents, mostly ornaments for everyone. Putting her hand into her pocket, she discovered to her dismay that her purse was missing.

Her eyes filled with tears as she excused herself from the counter in utter dismay, leaving the wrapped presents as she was unable to pay for them. Harry's hard-earned cash had gone, along with her key for the house. Frantically, she ran back the way she had come searching the ground as she ran and praying that her purse would be lying there somewhere. But her search was to no avail - it was gone forever, never to be seen again.

Extremely worried about what Harry would say, Ruth made her way home to find Jessie waiting as usual on the doorstep.

"Please, Jessie, can I come in until Harry gets home? I've lost my purse with the keys in," she said, then promptly burst into tears.

"Nay, lass, don't upset yourself so much. I'm sure Harry will understand," said Jessie, putting her puny little arms around Ruth to console her.

"Come on now, you're going to upset the baby if you continue to cry."

It was as Jessie had said; Harry understood.

"It just means that we won't be able to give presents this year, but I am sure they'll understand when we explain," said Harry, consoling her with a kiss.

Christmas approached fast, and Ruth was so happy for it had more meaning this year with the birth of their child. Ruth marvelled at the amazement in her daughter's eyes on seeing the fairy lights on their tree and in the streets and shops.

This happiness, however, was not to last. On the final week before Christmas, Ruth had arranged to meet Elizabeth to do their last-minute shopping.

As she set out for town, she thought that Beverley did not seem her normal happy little self, but put this down to the fact that the baby was teething. When most of the shopping was done, Ruth and her sister decided to have a meal in the town. Ruth sat at a table along with the shopping and her child whilst Elizabeth went to the counter to order their meals. The baby started to cry, so Ruth picked her up and gave her a cuddle, but found that she could not console her as usual. The child persisted in crying so much that they abandoned their meals and decided to leave for home. On arrival at home after a very fraught journey with the child persistently crying, Ruth gave her a feed, hoping that it would settle her to sleep. Ruth was quite perturbed when the child immediately pumped the feed back like a fountain, the force of which ejected it all over Ruth.

This happened at the next feed, also after persistent crying. Ruth by this time was extremely worried about the child. She phoned the doctor, who came in a very short time and informed her that the child had contacted gastroenteritis.

Ruth realised in horror where she had got it. The previous week, Ruth and the child had visited Harry's sister, who had a small boy of two who was not well. He had been sick that morning on a number of occasions while she was there, which had only been for about three-quarters of an hour. Neither her sister-in-law nor herself had realised that it was contagious.

The following day Ruth watched in horror at the deterioration in her baby's health. The child was continually sick and a terrible, brown, evil-smelling bowel movement was also starting to occur at intervals too regular for her liking. The motions were thin and steaming each time the baby passed them, but the worst thing was the pathetic cry from her baby's lips each time it happened, tearing her heart to breaking point, for she knew that the child was in terrible pain. Nothing she did for the child helped or gave her any comfort at all. As the tears fell from Ruth's eyes, she prayed fervently that her child could recover.

"Please God, make her better," she repeated over and over again as she cradled her precious child in her arms whilst her heart was tearing asunder.

Beverley's crying persisted all day and night. Weary from lack of sleep, Harry set off for work, unable to help Ruth in her anguish. He found on his return in the evening that the child was no better. Ruth sat up all night whilst Harry tried to get some sleep, but to no avail. The baby cried persistently. With a heavy heart, he went to work the following morning, worried not only about the baby but also about Ruth. Her face was now showing the strain; her eyes so very sad. The mountains of washing caused by the child's vomiting and diarrhoea were hanging all over the house on lines hastily put up to try and dry it.

Ruth sat with the child in her arms, rocking her between the bouts of sickness for hour after hour. She was not eating herself, and lack of sleep gave her a ghostly face.

Finally, on the fourth night Harry just had to go to his bed as he was driving during the day and had realised his reactions had been very slow during the previous day. Ruth stayed downstairs rocking the baby, who was still crying, but now very weakly.

The lack of sleep was telling on Ruth as she sat rocking. Her eyes were heavy and her head ached. Maybe if she lay down, the baby might settle a little. Gently she carried the child upstairs and laid her in her carrycot beside the now sleeping Harry. In a matter of seconds, Ruth fell asleep despite the crying baby by her side.

On that bitterly cold Christmas Eve morning, Ruth finally awoke to hear sobbing. Looking into the cot for the baby, she saw it empty and realised that the sobbing was coming from Harry. She dashed across to the landing, where Harry stood under the light.

The tears were falling uncontrollably from his eyes onto his white cheek as he cradled the baby in his arms.

Ruth knew instantly that Beverly was dead.

Harry never said a word as she took the baby, their firstborn, from his arms.

In sheer desperation, Ruth shook the baby as if willing her to come back to life but the baby's eyes remained fixed in the look of death. A small trickle of blood ran slowly down from the rosebud mouth that five days before had been smiling, but would never smile again.

Words cannot adequately express the despair and utter heartbreak that the pair of them felt as they stood in shocked silence, gazing into their dead child's face. Ruth cradled Beverly with her heart now shattered into fragments of grief, the child's body ice cold, and the tiny eyes so expressionless.

Why, dear God, did it have to happen? This child was loved so very much; she had brought such happiness into their lives, and now she lay motionless in her mother's arms. Her first Christmas presents were scattered around the house, wrapped in gaily-coloured paper; the tree they had so carefully trimmed stood in the corner of the room.

Ruth's broken heart and tired mind thought, *how meaningless it all is now - all the joy lost forever. Where indeed is God?* she asked herself, *and why has he forsaken us?*

'You look so peaceful lying there without a worry or a care

With tiny, soft pink fingers curled
The sweetest thing in all the world
A baby fresh as morning dew
A dainty flower with eyes of blue and rosy lips and creamy skin
Wee perfect nails, a dimpled chin
The gift of God from heaven above
Created by the hand of love.'

Patience strong

Gone forever.

Ruth had never before experienced death. The impact was tremendous; her whole world had collapsed. The coroner arrived with a policeman after Harry informed the doctor of the baby's death. Ruth felt numb as they wrapped the child in a blanket in front of her, covering the child completely. She wanted to say, "don't cover her face," but no sound came from her mouth.

She and Harry were asked to accompany the policeman and the coroner to the hospital. Ruth's mind was in chaos. Did they think that they had killed the child? Why the policeman? How could they think she could do such a terrible thing? These thoughts were racing through her head as she climbed into the back of the car with Harry.

She watched as the policeman laid the child between him and the coroner. His lips were moving, but she could not hear anything he was saying.

Ruth was oblivious as to what happened in the next hour, but she realised she was back home and Harry was talking to her.

"I have to go to work, Ruth. I have the main gate keys. They won't be able to get the wagons out if I don't go hand them in. Will you be all right, love, until I get back?"

Ruth nodded as she went to the door with him. After Harry left, she sat on the doorstep in a daze. Now the tears were falling uncontrollably down her face and she could hear the baby crying in her imagination as she sobbed her heart out alone.

The weather was bitterly cold and the snowflakes began to fall, mingling with the tears on her lap. There she sat, not wanting to go into the empty house, willing Harry to come back.

By the time he did, she was blue with cold. He gently picked her up and carried her into the house. They stood for a long time, huddled together, trying to get some warmth into her, then he gently put her into a chair and went to make a strong hot cup of tea for them both.

After a while, he helped her move Beverly's things into what was to have been her bedroom, shutting the door tightly, neither of them able to bear looking at her belongings.

The tree, complete with trimmings, also was moved, along with all the cards and paraphernalia of Christmas.

"I've phoned my parents, Ruth. My father has helped me to make arrangements for the funeral, but it will have to be delayed because they have to have a post mortem first."

Ruth looked at him but he was not sure she had understood what he had said, so he left it at that for the time being.

Later that day, Ruth went to see her parents to tell them their grandchild was dead, but they were not at home. So she returned home to find her father-in-law and Harry's brother waiting for her. Harry informed her that her parents had been visiting her with the Christmas presents whilst she was visiting them. They had been very shocked at the sad news, and had left.

"You don't have to stay here over Christmas alone – you're coming home with us until the funeral," Harry's father said.

Ruth obeyed without a murmur.

The following morning Ruth awoke from a troubled night's sleep of exhaustion and her hand accidentally brushed against Harry's face, which was ice cold. For a brief moment she was filled with panic and shuddered. The thought had been ridiculous. But she knew that her mind had played a peculiar trick in the state of shock she was in. Of course Harry was not dead.

Christmas time passed in a very sad household that year, the silence at times almost too much to bear.

Ruth could still hear the baby crying in her imagination as she lay awake hour after hour, tears falling onto her pillow silently as she lay.

The day of the funeral day arrived almost too quickly. Harry gently took Ruth's hand as they entered their home again for the first time since the death. Ruth visibly shook from head to toe as they went in.

Silently, they waited for the undertaker to bring their child home for the last time. At ten thirty, the black car arrived with the tiny white coffin containing the precious child's body.

"The baby's here, Ruth," Harry said, turning to his sad wife whose face had turned chalk-white with red-ringed eyes. "You stay here and I'll go to the door."

Gently the coffin was carried in and placed on tiny trestles in front of the window. As the undertaker took the lid off, Ruth rose to her feet to look at her child.

She said not a word as she gazed at the tiny body before her.

Beverley was dressed all in white satin, edged with delicate pink lace around her face. A tiny rosebud had been placed on her chest. She looked so peaceful and pretty that Ruth felt a little peace in her heartbreak and grief as the undertaker took his leave.

Harry tenderly placed his arms around his wife's shoulders and together they stood looking at the baby, neither of them speaking a word. Each was lost in private thoughts and silent grief.

The flowers began to arrive. There were so many beautiful tributes from people they did not even know. Word of the baby's death had flown around the village, thanks to Jessie and Amy, who were also beside themselves with grief.

The entire village had been touched by the sad news, judging by the number of posies: teddies made of flowers; baskets and flowers of all descriptions arrived constantly.

Beautiful letters of sympathy were also hand-delivered; it seemed the whole village was in mourning with them.

Both sets of parents arrived, but still Ruth remained silent, her eyes transfixed on the tiny coffin.

Jessie handed her a cup of tea whilst Ruth sat stroking her child's face gently with her shaking hand, feeling nothing but an intense hurt searing into her soul.

The time for the funeral had arrived.

"Come and sit over here, Ruth," Harry pleaded as the undertaker moved over to where the child lay. Ruth obeyed as in a trance. Slowly the lid was lifted and placed over the baby before being fastened down for the last time. As each screw turned, Ruth felt as if a knife were being slowly pushed into her own body as she watched. The snow began to gently fall as they left, as if the angels were crying for the lost child.

Ruth had never before seen a dead body or attended a funeral; she was completely unaware of the devastating effect it was to have on her. The memory of the minute coffin being slowly lowered into the deep cold grave was to torment her sleep for weeks after. The child was laid to rest under the watchful eyes of an angel monument on the grave behind hers.

At last the dreadful day was over as Ruth wearily crawled into bed that night to eventually fall into a fitful sleep of exhaustion, only to be awakened from a nightmare in the early hours of the morning. She was screaming out loud in a cold sweat, digging with all her might at the bedclothes with her hands, trying to stop the worms eating into her daughter's coffin.

Mercifully, the passage of time turned the horror of her loss into an ever-present but dull pain that eventually became tolerable, the day-to-day functions of life taking over again. The hurt healed slightly yet the memory of it remained, her life changed forever by the will of God for some reason known only to him. To Ruth and Harry, this reason was a mystery and one they could well have done without. United in their grief, they knew they had to start again on a new path of life together.

Beverley's death had left a vast emptiness in their lives, but each knew they had to pick up the threads and start again.

A few weeks later on a visit to her parents' home, Ruth was appalled at her father's remarks.

"It's probably for the best, lass; you can start all over again. Have another baby later, but in the meantime put some money behind you."

How dare he say such a thing? How could he be so callous? Had he no feelings? Her eyes blazed with anger as she picked up her coat and looked at her father.

"I would gladly give all I had in the world to hold my living child in my arms again and see her smile," she said, and with that she left the house. So much for his support. *Please God, don't let me get as hard as he is,* she prayed as she marched home furiously.

1959

Harry had changed his job during the spring months. He had joined his mate selling washing machines on a commission basis and spent many evenings working late on his rounds.

Ruth became very lonely on an evening after her day's work at the local mill, where they made tartan cloth and kilts for export.

Harry bought her a television set, so she invited Amy and Jessie round to view it with her several evenings a week. She also kept up with the gossip that way.

"Did you know that they've sent Mrs Conway's husband to jail again?" enquired Jessie on one such evening.

"He never learns, does he?" replied Amy "All those children living on social security again. I don't think he cares."

"How many have they now?" Ruth asked with a frown. "I'm sure it's about eight or nine, all under ten years of age, the youngest of which is just crawling. I see her regularly crawling near the front door next to the main road and my heart leaps into my throat and fairly misses a beat seeing her so near to danger. She has the face of an angel underneath that dirt, but her clothes are always ragged and dirty."

The child's mother was young and constantly screamed at the children, often leaving them alone at night for hours on end.

Ruth could not help the feeling of bitterness that would creep over her at the thought of her beloved child, snatched from her in a matter of days, yet here was a woman that did not care. Children locked in a home without love.

Life was so unfair. They were such beautiful children, with fair hair and eyes like pools of blue water. Their mother had no idea what treasures she had been entrusted with and Ruth constantly asked herself over and over again, " Why?"

The whole of that summer was a series of mishaps, starting with the end house of the block almost being demolished.

A steep incline ended at the corner junction of the road on which Ruth lived, the end house having its door across the corner. On the opposite side of the road the river made its slow progress, rippling gently over stones as it passed the mill where Ruth worked.

The road had been made as a bypass for the town centre. It was always a very busy road, used by a constant stream of heavy goods vehicles loaded to the top with all sorts of heavy haulage, from machinery to crates, car transporters and articulated vehicles which created constant noise. Each one was heading for the motor way en route to their various destinations around the countryside. Many a time a squeal of brakes could be heard as a driver tried to negotiate the bend a little too fast.

One such time, however, a driver did not succeed. He misjudged the bend and with an almighty bang ended up in the front room of a house, after demolishing half the front wall and the doorway. He sat in his cab with the stonework all around him and the terrified occupant in a state of shock. No one was seriously hurt, however; just badly shocked, but the householder was not too pleased at the state of her home.

The next episode struck Ruth as being quite funny. She was standing in front of the room window, looking out onto the road whilst buttering bread for the tea on a warm sunny afternoon in mid summer. Harry was sitting behind her in his armchair reading the paper. During the week, the council had dug the road up leaving a large hole, piling the stones and rubble into a large mound beside it. They were to lay new sewage pipes, as the old ones were outdated.

The river across the road was slowly rippling along its way, the trees full of lush green leaves and the banking alive with buttercups, dandelions and daisies. The sun was quite warm, blazing brightly from a blue sky with only an occasional cloud drifting by.

She heard the motorcycle before she could see it, its slow hum whining away in the distance. Looking up from the table she saw the birds rising from the riverbank and the motorcyclist appearing in view.

Ruth could not believe her eyes when the motorcyclist, complete with bike, disappeared in to the hole. She exploded into laughter, causing Harry to look up from his reading. He thought she had gone crazy; the strain of the previous months showing at last, maybe.

Ruth was unable to speak as she was laughing so hysterically, the tears rolling down her face. Each time she stopped laughing to try and tell Harry about it, she would begin again.

Holding her aching stomach, the laughter continuing, she got hold of Harry and dragged him to the door. Still laughing uncontrollably, she led him to the hole where the dazed driver was lying underneath his bike.

Harry was horrified to see the poor soul desperately trying to get out, whilst in the meantime his wife was still laughing. He apologised to the man and leaned over into the hole to assist. With great difficulty, he managed to pull him out. The poor man was unhurt but very badly shaken.

Ruth finally managed to stop laughing and asked the man to forgive her. Together they assisted him into the house, where Ruth put the kettle on and Harry tried to clean him up a little.

"I shall go and inspect the damage whilst you drink your tea," Harry said, leaving Ruth to apologise for her rudeness.

"I really am sorry," Ruth said as she handed him the tea, "but you must see the funny side of it. I couldn't help it - one minute you were riding along the road in broad daylight, the next minute you'd disappeared from view. It was like watching a cartoon on the telly."

She smiled at him, somewhat embarrassed, and asked if he was hurt in any way.

The stranger smiled as he took the tea from Ruth with shaking hands.

"It's all right lass," he said. "I understand. The sun blinded me for a moment and I didn't see the hole 'until it was too late to do anything about it. I just hope my bike is Ok, as I haven't finished paying for it yet."

As he finished speaking Harry re-entered the room, his face

smudged with grease and dust.

"Can't get the bike out without a rope, I'm afraid," he told the stranger. "Perhaps you can give me a hand when you've got over your fright, sir."

'There's no rush," Ruth told him. "Let the gentleman drink his tea and stop shaking. I'll go and find that old clothesline I put away in case we ever needed a rope for anything. Lucky I did, don't you think?"

On her return she handed Harry the rope. "Will it be strong enough do you think?" she asked.

"Yes, that will be fine. We can double it up a few times. I think this will do the trick, don't you, sir?" he asked of the man, who by now had composed himself a little.

It took the three of them quite a while to get the rope tied around the bike before it could be lifted from the hole, with Harry in the hole taking the weight and pushing while the other two tried to pull from the top.

When eventually the job was completed, Harry's face was like a beetroot with sweat running down his cheeks and mingling with the grease and dust. His shirt was torn and he had scraped his hands in a number of places.

"Come inside now," Ruth told the pair of them. "I'll get a wet cloth to clean you both up and get you a cold drink."

The weary pair followed her into the house and sank exhaustedly into chairs.

"I really am most obliged to you both for your assistance and kindness," the rider said as he accepted the wet cloth from Ruth. "I would never have managed to get the bike out on my own, I'm sure."

Ruth handed him a glass of dandelion and burdock.

"Don't think anything about it, sir" she replied. " I had a good laugh at your expense, the best I've had for a long time. It's sure to have done me good. I was just about to prepare our tea when it happened; you're more than welcome to share it with us if you would like to."

Putting down his empty glass, the man thanked Ruth.

"Nay, lass, I've been enough trouble to you and your hubby this afternoon without imposing further on your hospitality. Thank you once again, but I must really be on my way. My wife will think I've got lost on the moors somewhere. I've been out all day giving the bike a good run but I usually get home about mid-afternoon, so now I'm about two hours late. My wife will be just about ready for calling the police by the time I get home and sending a search party out for me. Cheerio then, much obliged".

With a cheery smile he climbed onto the bike, putting on the dented crash helmet and probably thinking to himself that it was a good job he'd been wearing it. He turned, giving a wave as he disappeared into the distance, the bike looking none the worse for its tumble.

Harry and Ruth turned to each other and laughed.

"It was good to see you laughing again, Ruth, my love," said Harry. "It seems such a long time since I've seen you with even a smile on your face." He lovingly took her into his arms after closing the door.

THE SIXTIES

Many things were happening in the world during the decade leading up to the seventies. Once more there was nearly full employment. Jobs were very easy to get; the local evening papers were inundated with job advertisements night after night.

Money was also easily available to many as loans, but not as easy to pay off due to the amount of interest that would be added before the final payment.

The population erupted with a baby boom and the swinging sixties had begun.

Mary Quant burst onto the fashion scene of Carnaby Street and the Kings Road in mini skirts, hot pants, thigh boots and tights.

Out went stockings and suspenders - no longer sensible with mini skirts, much to the delight of girls everywhere, fed up of sitting on buttons digging into bare thighs. No wonder there was a baby boom! With so much leg on display, every boy's blood was racing as he watched the girls go by on platform soles that made them look two or three inches taller.

In came the Beatles: John, Paul, Ringo and George, with the Liverpool sound. Four young teenage boys with the right sound in music, girls going crazy at the mere mention of their names, standing for hours in all weather to catch a glimpse of them, screaming their heads off in delight and passing out in the crush to touch one of them.

Everywhere was Beatle mania - the same four smiling faces on T shirts, posters, wallpaper, magazines, cups, beakers - literally everywhere you looked. The four teenagers were well on their way to becoming millionaires.

Out went the teddy boys with their thick, crepe-soled shoes and greasy, slicked-back hair; their drainpipe trousers and long jackets.

The Beatles were tidy-looking - the 'boy next door' kind of look - and even the mums approved of them. Many more stars came from the Liverpool area, but none were as popular as the Beatles.

It was during this time that Ruth applied for a job. She felt very bored with Harry away all day at work. Since the death of Beverley, she had desperately wanted another child but had on two occasions miscarried in the early months. Between them they had decided not to keep hoping for another child for the time being and decided that Ruth would try for a job to keep her occupied and boost their income for a while.

After a successful interview at the local chemical works, Ruth was to start the following month in the comptometer section of the wages department. Her job was to work out the bonus pay for the shift workers, based on an index of special letters and numbers representing various pay amounts which was added to their basic wage at the end of the month.

She soon learnt how to do this and quite liked the job, even though it was a little repetitive. The office was cheery and her fellow workmates helped her over the initial stages of learning if she got stuck. Ruth was receiving quite a good salary every month and things were looking up at last for them, with more money available for extras.

Harry started to go out for a drink with his fellow workmates on the odd evening now and again.

Ruth could hardly dare to hope that her suspicions were right, when a few months later she thought that she could be pregnant again. Much to her dismay, however, Harry was not too pleased when she told him it was possible. The time was much too soon according to Harry; they were just getting on their feet and he was enjoying a bit of pleasure for the first time since they had married.

Just under eight months later, whether Harry liked it or not, Ruth got her wish. Their second child was born after a difficult labour for Ruth, the baby having to be delivered with forceps and Ruth promptly going into shock. The baby did not have an easy time of it either. Her tiny face was bruised and there was a lump on her head which was to last for six weeks, giving her a funny-shaped head.

Ruth was happy and Harry seemed to be, as he held his new baby in his arms at last.

Anne Marie was a happy child, making Ruth feel complete again. Harry loved his new daughter, but not in the same way as he had loved Beverly. He still went out for his pint with the boys, sometimes more often than he should.

After Anne Marie reached her second birthday, Ruth was once again pregnant and realised that this time the house would be too small when the new baby arrived.

After visiting the council offices, they were offered two different houses but neither was suitable and they turned them down due to the state of disrepair. The third time they were lucky; the house was just what they wanted. A long garden surrounded by a fence sloped away from the house, leading to a deep drop, the banking of which led to the railway line.

Harry decided it was quite safe for the children as there were plenty of trees and bushes planted just behind the fence alongside bramble bushes to deter any trespassers. These would stop their children getting anywhere near the banking and the steep drop. It might also be fun watching the trains going along their merry way to the station in the town, or going the other way for a trip elsewhere.

The house was the end of a block of four, with six steps leading to a side door. On entering, the staircase ran from a small hallway up to the floor above. On either side of the stairs were two doors, one leading into the rather large kitchen, the other to the front room. The house was immaculately clean, which Ruth appreciated very much as she had only four weeks to go before the birth date. The wallpaper was clean but not really to Ruth's taste; however, that could wait until after the birth.

"We'll move in this weekend," Harry said to Ruth, as she busied her self looking in all the kitchen cupboards.

"I've never had a kitchen like this, Harry. It will be lovely to work in here during the day, then sit in the lounge in the evening. I think I shall have it painted blue when the time comes to decorate."

"Oh, give us a chance, lass. We have to get over our broken sleep first every night for the next few weeks with the new baby."

"I know, love. I didn't mean straightaway - I was just planning ahead," Ruth replied with a cheeky grin.

For the next three weeks Ruth busied herself as best she could, arranging the house and preparing things for the new arrival.

Anne Marie spent most of her time running from one room to another with her toys. The garden got a little attention from Harry when he had the time, digging a small vegetable patch and cutting the overgrown lawn.

Ruth managed to sweep the paths, but with her cumbersome shape she found it very hard work

"I think we'll have a rockery here, Harry. I think it would look nice, don't you?"

"Yes, love. I'll get some stones for you from the banking in a minute when I've finished this lawn."

Within the hour the rockery began to take shape, Harry doing the hard work and Ruth planting small plants from elsewhere in the garden, hoping for them to spread and give ground cover in a short time.

"I hope it rains tonight to water them in," Ruth said wistfully, "then I shan't have to keep watering the plants to get them established."

"It certainly looks like it could," Harry replied. "Look at the black clouds coming over."

Rain it did, as a deafening roll of thunder startled them both an hour later. Then large, penny-sized drops began to fall fast and furious.

"Good! That's what we want, Ruth," Harry said, looking out of the window. "Just the thing for starting the vegetable plot and the rockery. It's much better for the garden than tap water that's been treated, and saves us a lot of work also, thank goodness."

Starting the garden was not the only thing to happen that day.

Ruth went into labour in the evening, and the following day was their wedding anniversary.

Ruth kindly obliged by presenting Harry with another daughter a week earlier than expected. This time it was much easier and she had no trouble. Mother and baby Tracy were both fine.

"That's three girls I've given birth to. I don't think I can breed boys, do you?" Ruth asked the midwife laughingly.

"Maybe next time, luvvy," she replied with a grin.

"Gosh! I don't think we want another baby after this one, thank you," replied Ruth, shaking her head. "Harry wasn't too pleased with this time or the last. He wanted us to wait for a while before starting a family, but what will be will, be don't you think?"

"Aye, luvvy, that's right. There's nowt we can do about it."

Ruth settled down to rearing her family very happily. The house was lovely, the garden blooming and the vegetables were harvested. The room had been decorated to their taste, also the kitchen and upstairs, making it all look homely. She spent the day after the housework was done walking or playing with the children.

Ruth visited Mary quite often. By now she had two children, the second of whom was a girl. They took it in turns to visit each other's homes on a weekly basis. The older children played quite happily while the two of them chatted merrily away, drinking coffee and comparing the antics the children had got up to since their last visit. Mary had moved into a brand new house, much larger than Ruth's and further into the country. Often they would take the children for a walk in the afternoons to the local recreation ground so they could play on the swings and enjoy good, clean, fresh air away from the traffic fumes.

It was nearing the end of summer. Autumn was fast approaching and winter would soon be on its way. The weather was starting to turn cool. All too soon, it would be unpleasant to go out in the afternoon with the young ones, so they enjoyed it as much as possible while they had the chance. Ruth was happy.

All was right in her world.

1960 TO 1970

Christmas 1963 was fast approaching when at lunchtime on November 23rd Ruth switched on the television set to see if there was anything suitable for Anne Marie to watch.

She stood rooted to the spot in disbelief and shock. Tears came into her eyes as she watched the horror before her eyes on the screen. A report from America, November 22^{nd,} USA time.

"John F Kennedy has been shot," the reporter screamed.

One second before, the President of the United States of America had been shown driving through Dallas in his motorcade surrounded by security guards. His beautiful wife Jackie sat beside him smiling, on their way to lunch. The next second the President had slumped against his wife, who immediately tried to scramble over the back seat of the moving vehicle in terror.

Pandemonium erupted all around, security men dashing everywhere. No one could believe what they had seen with their own eyes. One minute the crowd had been cheering and waving flags, the President smiling and waving along with his wife to their supporters; the next minute everyone was looking stunned.

Was the president dead? Or just injured? No one knew for sure.

John F Kennedy had been inaugurated as the thirty-fifth President of the United States on January 20th, 1961. He was the youngest man ever to be elected as President, a young man with new ideas for America. Well-liked with his boyish good looks and dazzling smile, he had a passion for civil rights.

After the incident he was rushed to the Parkland Medical Centre, later to be pronounced dead. His apparent assassin, an ex-marine by the name of Lee Harvey Oswald, was arrested. He never stood trial for the President's assassination, as he himself was to be assassinated by Jack Ruby two day later. Ruby himself died some time later from stomach cancer.

The President's lifeless body was loaded onto a plane for the return journey to Washington.

The Vice President, Lyndon B Johnson, was sworn in during the flight. On the twenty-fifth, John F Kennedy was laid to rest at the Arlington National Cemetery after being transported there in the very hearse that Abraham Lincoln had used ninety-eight years before. The funeral was televised worldwide.

The killer, or killers, of the President were never proven or brought to justice.

Other notable events in the sixties were the war in Vietnam, the assassination of the former President's brother, Robert, and there was Martin Luther King, the civil rights leader.

Back in the United Kingdom, Donald Campbell died attempting to break the world water speed record on Lake Coniston in the Lake District.

The wartime Prime Minister, Sir Winston Churchill, died at the age of ninety on January 24th, seventy years to the day after his father Lord Randolph had died.

In 966 a tiny Welsh mining village called Aberfan awoke as usual on a normal day like any other; a dull morning with rain. The children were attending their local school when at nine fifteen precisely a coal tip suddenly began to move, smashing the canal pipes on its way. It sent water and slurry to create a great wave, higher than a house, gushing down the valley.

No one saw the menacing heap as it slid mercilessly on its way. A complete farm, a row of houses, a village junior school - all were totally engulfed by the sea of murderous thick, black slurry. One hundred and sixteen children, together with five teachers and twenty-three others, were asphyxiated or drowned without any warning. It was the last day of school before the half term holiday.

A whole generation of children was wiped out in one swift move, an inexplicable act of God. As the village mourned, the television showed the devastation.

Ruth was stunned by the reports, weeping alongside the parents as they were interviewed. Her heart went out to them, and to one mother in particular who had said that she had been cross with her child before sending him off to school that fatal morning. Her last words to her son had been in anger.

"How I wish I could turn the clock back and cuddle him before he left!" the mother cried in her anguish.

What a useless waste of young lives, thought Ruth. *Why do these things have to happen? Is it God's wrath on a wicked world?*

Such heartbreak over innocent children.

The earth was not the only place in the news. The moon had been under study for some time, scientists doing their best to try and discover ways of visiting it. At last they had achieved what had previously been thought impossible.

A man had eventually landed on the moon. Neil Armstrong was to be immortalised as the first man to step on the moon in nineteen sixty-nine. Thanks to the wonders of modern science, the world saw the event through their television sets.

"One step for man, a giant leap for mankind," were Armstrong's words on stepping from the spacecraft to place an American ensign into the moon's surface, watched by millions in their own homes.

What a Decade!

A SON AT LAST

Another page in Ruth's diary of life was about to unfold.

Harry was a little upset when she told him he was to be a father yet again. Anne Marie was nicely settled in school; Tracy had just turned three and was about to start at nursery school. Harry had been half-hoping that Ruth would get a part time job whilst the children were at school, but now this would not be possible.

The months were passing too slowly for Ruth. She did not feel quite right about this pregnancy; something seemed to be amiss.

Harry became a little more pleased at the thought that this time it may be a son. He still was spending a lot of time away at night, drinking with the boys, much to Ruth's dismay. She herself spent a lot of time knitting for the girls and the new baby. Then the one thing she had dreaded happened, and she began to miscarry again.

"Oh Goodness! Where's Harry? I need the doctor. The girls are in bed - the phone is up the road - he's never here when I need him!" she cried aloud.

Slowly she dragged herself to the next door neighbours'.

"Please, get me the doctor," she pleaded.

But all was not lost.

"If you're careful and rest, you should be able to keep the baby," the doctor told her when he had examined her.

The months passed and Ruth was still pregnant, but all was still not quite right as the baby was lying in the breach position.

"You'll have to come to the clinic to see the specialist," her doctor informed her at her pre-natal check up. "Your baby is lying with its head under your rib cage; that's why you feel the discomfort you've talked about. I'll make an appointment for Monday next for you."

As Ruth lay on the examination couch in the specialist's clinic, her heart was sad. *Why is it such trouble to bring my family into the world?* she thought. The doctor gripped the baby with both hands, turning as he did so. She felt the baby move round, only to move back again as soon as he released his hold. He tried again, making her stomach feel rather sore, but it was no good - the baby spun back yet again.

"That's it for today, Ruth," he said. "We'll try again next week. We still have plenty of time - the baby's not due for another nine weeks yet."

She rose and dressed herself, feeling very tender around her stomach. Slowly and feeling very despondent, she left the clinic.

The girls were in bed and Harry was out as usual when she felt a great urge to visit the loo. Slowly she climbed the stairs; it was such an effort tonight. Her neighbour popped in whilst she was upstairs.

"I shan't be long," she called to Mags. "Pop the kettle on please, for a coffee. I'll be down in a minute."

They never got the coffee, for to Ruth's horror the bathroom floor started to cover with blood.

"Help me!" she screamed. Mags came running faster than Ruth had ever seen her move before.

"Oh my God, Ruth, you're haemorrhaging. Lie down flat straight away," she shouted as she dashed to get some bath towels from the airing cupboard. "I'll get an ambulance."

"No, get Harry. He's at the pub and it's nearer than the ambulance station," Ruth shouted back.

Harry came, but arrived with a mate.

"I'll just drop Jim off at his home on the way to the hospital," were the first words he said to her.

Ruth could not believe what he was saying, but was to tired to argue. By the time they got to the Casualty Department, Ruth was deathly white and the towels which had been hastily packed around her body by Mags were soaked with blood. She was rushed into the doctor, shaking more with fright than anything else. She was admitted straight away.

"You must stay flat on your back until the bleeding stops," the nurse informed her. "There is still a chance that your baby will survive this trauma and be born quite naturally if you're lucky."

Five weeks later Ruth was discharged, still pregnant. She was tired of lying around doing nothing for days and days on end, but it had been worth it as she could now expect a normal delivery at the end of the month, the doctor had reassured her as she left that morning.

"Harry, we must go to the town as I have to get the baby essentials that I need. There's a market on today - we might get some bargains," Ruth said hopefully.

"All right then," Harry said, not too enthusiastically, but off they went.

The day was hot and the market crowded. Ruth had backache and wished she had stayed at home, but dared not say so. She realised that the shopping had to be done to give her time to wash everything in preparation for the birth. They managed to get everything that was needed and at last they were ready to go home.

Harry had changed his job a few months before; he was working for himself as a decorator and he was doing quite well and getting plenty of work.

He told Ruth to wait while he took the shopping to the car and said he would pick her up at the entrance to the market to stop her having to battle through the crowds. He was away rather along time, so Ruth decided to go and look for him. She found him talking to a dark-haired woman, younger than herself and quite pretty in a rough sort of way.

Harry introduced her to the woman as a customer he was working for, then taking their leave they eventually arrived at the car. She sank gratefully into the seat next to him, her back aching, her feet swollen and her head swimming.

After a rest and a quick tea, Ruth inspected her shopping.

"I'll wash these tomorrow," she said to Harry. "I'm too tired now."

Mags popped in to see what she had bought.

"You look terrible, Ruth. Do you feel all right?" she asked.

"Not really," replied Ruth, "but I'm sure I'll feel better when the girls are in bed and I can put my feet up."

Mags gave her a hand with the girls and left, promising to call in later to see how she was after a rest.

Ruth made herself a cup of tea and sat on the sofa with her feet up on a cushion. *That's better,* she thought. *I'm very tired, but the shopping had to be done. I'm glad I did it today, as I won't be feeling any better the nearer the birth I get.*

An hour later Ruth awoke to the sound of Mags closing the door.

"I must have fallen asleep," she said laughingly to her neighbour.

"Well! You must have needed it," replied Mags. "I'll put the kettle on, shall I, because your last cup of tea must be stone cold by now. Look at the skin on the top of it!"

Together they spent the rest of the evening chattering about the girls and the expected baby. Harry had gone to the pub as usual after the girls were settled for the night and Ruth was a little annoyed at him as she thought he was being a bit inconsiderate, considering her state of health.

Ruth awoke during the night to visit the bathroom, feeling as though she were starting in labour.

"Oh dear, not yet! It's too soon," she said to herself. But two hours later she knew it was so.

"Harry, wake up please. It's time to go to the hospital."

The baby made its entrance into the world at five thirty in the morning. The words were ringing in Ruth's ears:

"It's a boy!"

He had arrived five weeks early weighing three and a half pounds. Ruth was settled in the ward enjoying a well-earned cup of tea, a glow of satisfaction shining from her eyes.

"I have a son for Harry. Thank You, Lord."

Harry visited her as soon as he was able after attending to the girls. Shortly after his departure, the specialist baby doctor visited Ruth. He sat beside Ruth on the bed.

"I have to tell you, dear, that your baby is not very well. We have had to take him into the intensive care unit."

Ruth stared at him in disbelief.

"But you said he was fine, a good weight for a premature baby!" The tears began to well in her eyes. "No, this cannot be happening!"

"I'm extremely sorry, dear, but it is. His lungs collapsed shortly after we washed him and put him in the nursery. We'd like to baptise him as soon as possible. I'll send the vicar to see you later. At the moment we've inserted a tube into his lungs to drain the fluid that has collected in them while you were carrying. As soon as he started to breathe, his lungs punctured like an over-inflated balloon. I'm afraid he also has some problem with his kidneys but we won't know the extent of the damage until we do a special X- ray. First we must get his lungs functioning properly before we can attempt to do the test. He has to be able to breathe on his own for at least five hours after we remove the tube."

All colour had drained from Ruth's face as she stared at the doctor, the tears rolling down her face in a torrent and soaking her nightgown.

"Please can I see him?" she pleaded.

"I'll send a nurse for you with a wheelchair to take you up into the intensive care baby unit. You realise that you'll have to look at him through the glass, as it is a sterile area? I'll arrange for the vicar to meet you there, Ruth. We can then baptize him at the same time if that's all right with you."

Ruth nodded her agreement.

Andrew was baptised whilst still lying in his incubator. Two nurses, the doctor and the vicar accompanied Ruth, but Harry was absent.

This was not as she had imagined her child's baptism to be, and though the other people were present, Ruth felt so terribly alone, her heart sad as she gazed at the tiny infant wrapped in padding with tubes up his nose and more in his chest. Tiny discs were attached to his chest, connected to a monitor recording his heartbeats. His eyes were shut.

She wanted, needed, so very much to hold him, to cradle him in her arms and make everything all right for him. No sound came from the infant; just the bleep of the monitor to prove he was still alive.

On her return to the ward, the sound of laughter and cheerful voices invaded her mind as she fought back the tears that threatened to overwhelm her. The lusty cry of hungry babies tore at her heart.

"What have I done to deserve this? Why is my baby so ill? Dear God, help us all!" she pleaded in utter despair. "Please, please save our son."

The days slipped by agonisingly slowly as Andrew clung by a slender thread to life. To help Ruth, the doctor agreed that she could express her breast milk to enable the nursing staff to feed him through the tube, as it would be more beneficial for him. It made it easier for her not being around while the other mothers fed their babies. It also made her feel not quite so helpless in the battle for his fragile life. The tube to his lungs was removed time and time again, but always had to be replaced when he failed to breathe on his own. Ruth visited the intensive care at any hour and any opportunity she had. Unable to touch the tiny bundle, she clung to the incubator side in desperation, praying constantly.

Harry did not seem to feel the enormity of the situation, despite being told by Ruth and being kept well informed by the specialist. Ruth felt exceedingly perturbed by Harry's apparent lack of concern for his desperately ill son. There also was a lack of support for her when she needed it most. She could not understand his attitude at all; it worried her greatly.

The following days passed slowly, with her son improving one day only to relapse the day after. Ruth was allowed home but continued to visit each day to see her baby son. On one such visit the doctor told her he was going to try injecting a dye through the child's veins and inspect by X-ray its progress through to his kidneys, about which they were becoming more and more concerned.

"Ring later today and we'll tell you what we find," the doctor informed her on her departure.

"The results are not good," Ruth was told when she rang back later. "The baby has problems that require an immediate operation, and we are unable to carry it out with the facilities at this hospital."

Ruth shuddered at these words.

"He will have to be rushed to another town where they specialise in this kind of operation. Can you get here soon to accompany him, as they will need some of your blood in the theatre?"

Ruth threw on her coat in a panic and dashed off, after informing Harry what was happening and telling him he would have to see to the girls. She arrived at the ward just in time to see her son being wheeled in his incubator into the lift. The doctor and a sister accompanied him.

The child looked so tiny bundled up in cotton wool, tubes peeping out here and there. He was asleep and looked so peaceful, but it was the effect of the anaesthetic that he had been given previously. Together they entered the ambulance with the baby, the sister armed with a file of notes, to begin the journey.

Ruth felt an urgent desire to hold her tiny son as tears threatened to fall. She had held him for a brief moment at his birth before he had been taken away. Now it was impossible, as his life depended on the incubator. On arrival at the hospital, Ruth was parted from her son once again whilst he was taken to a cubicle. She was sent to the laboratory for the blood tests and to sign the consent form for her infant's operation. The formalities completed, Ruth was escorted to a sitting room to await the specialist's report following the operation. She sat for two hours whilst Andrew was in theatre, feeling so worried that she felt she would explode. Where was Harry? He should have been here by now.

The operation completed, the doctor entered the room and sat beside her.

"Now, my dear," he began. " The news is not good."

Ruth's heart missed a beat, the tears once more threatening.

"We cannot tell at this stage if our efforts have been successful. His urethral valves are not working correctly, and that is the reason why fluid built up in his body during your pregnancy. This in turn damaged his lungs, so that when he took his first breath they punctured. We have tried to correct these in theatre, but only time will tell if we have been successful. You may go home for now as there's no point waiting: he's under strict supervision in the intensive care wing. We'll ring you later. Goodbye, my dear."

Harry was waiting in the car park as she stepped out of the hospital. She told him what had happened but he said nothing, just started the car up and began to leave.

For two days her son was taken back and forth in and out of theatre. She had been asked not to visit. Waking from a troubled sleep on the third day by a knocking on the door, she rose, half expecting to see Mags at the door. Ruth opened the door to find a policeman on the doorstep.

"I've got a message for you. Can you ring the hospital as soon as possible, please?" Ruth knew immediately the reason for this request. She ran immediately to the phone

"Could you come to the hospital?" the voice on the phone was saying.

"Please, please tell me he's not dead," she cried.

"I'm sorry, we cannot give you any information over the phone. You must come to the hospital."

Hurriedly she dialled for Harry.

"Come home now!" she shouted into the mouthpiece.

The nightmare journey seemed to last forever until at last the hospital came into sight. Ruth ran into the ward.

"Sit down please, Ruth," the doctor said. "I'm sorry, but it's bad news. Andrew developed complications after the last operation and died peacefully in his sleep early this morning."

"I know, I know," she cried.

The doctor left Ruth and Harry alone with their thoughts, reappearing a short time later with two cups of tea.

"I have something to ask of you which may trouble you a great deal. Can we have your permission to donate Andrew's organs for medical research? We need organs desperately. It is most important, and may enable us to save other babies' lives at a later date.

After much thought Ruth and Harry gave their consent, Ruth's reason being that she did not want any other mother to feel the way she herself was feeling at that moment.

The death had to be registered in the town where it had occurred, so they had to wait for the details that were to go on the death certificate. The doctor eventually handed them the necessary documentation.

"Take these to the registrar," he said. "He will give you the certificates before you go home. Please may I express my deepest condolences to you both at this sad time."

Shaking hands with them both and giving Ruth a gentle pat on her shoulder, he took his leave.

Two days later the funeral arrangements had been made. Ruth was sitting alone whilst Harry was at the pub as usual. A deep depression had settled over Ruth; she was almost unaware of the presence of her two daughters in the home. Acting like a robot, she performed her motherly duties in a daze. Mags was a tower of strength for her. Harry had been no help whatsoever to Ruth, going about his daily work as usual and saying very little. Ruth thought it was his way of grieving. She herself felt very guilty due to the fact that Andrew had been born too early. If only she could have kept him warm and cosy inside her until the correct time, maybe everything would have been all right. She tormented herself constantly with these thoughts during the week leading up to the funeral and her nerves started to show the effects. Her hands shook uncontrollably and she was unable to sleep or eat, surviving only on cups of tea.

On the last evening before the dreaded day, Ruth was once more alone except for the sleeping girls when a knock came at the door. Ruth opened it to a slightly familiar face but could not place who it was. The woman was slim with dark hair, well dressed in high-heeled shoes and a suit.

"Hello Ruth," she said. "You don't know me, but I know Harry very well."

Ruth asked her into her home.

"I've known Harry for over twelve months," she said. "In fact, we've been going out together most of that time. While you were in the hospital, Harry stayed at my flat. I thought it was time you knew. I was hoping he would tell you himself, but obviously he hasn't judging by the look on your face."

Ruth continued looking at the woman in stunned silence. She remembered seeing her at the market. She could hardly believe her ears - this could not be happening; not when the funeral was to be in the morning. The woman told her many things about Harry and she knew about the baby. Ruth had had no idea about the affair. How could she have been so blind? That's where Harry was instead of the pub night after night. After the woman had left, Harry arrived home within the hour.

"I've just had a visitor," she told him.

"I know," he replied.

"Tell me it's not true, Harry, please. It can't be, can it?"

"Yes, I'm afraid it is, Ruth. I told her it was over because of the baby, but she doesn't want it to be and I'm not sure I do either."

"Harry, how could you?" she screamed at him.

"Lots of men do it," Harry shouted back, "so why not me?"

He slammed the door as he left and Ruth collapsed in tears. The girls were in bed sleeping as she decided to end this misery. It would be so easy; just turn on the gas and she would fall asleep, then it would be over. *First I must kiss the girls goodbye,* she thought, and slowly she climbed the stairs to their bedroom.

The children were sleeping so peacefully, unaware of the drama downstairs. She knelt beside their bed, and looking at them brought her back to sanity as she realised that if she did what she intended, her little girls could possibly die too. This she did not want.

"Oh dear God, no, don't let me do that to them," she begged aloud as she fell on her knees beside the sleeping girls.

"Please, Lord, help me through this terrible time," she prayed.

Ruth sat on the floor for a long time until she realised that Harry was not coming home for the night. Maybe he would come tomorrow, for his son was coming home for the first and last time.

He arrived just as the tiny white coffin was being brought into the room and stood on trestles. He said not a word to Ruth, but together they looked at their son lying there in peaceful rest. No wires or tubes now. Through her mind was running the thought, *I have held this child but once, now he is no more.* Gently, she bent to kiss him.

She had been told that he would have been ill all his life had he lived, but it was little help in her anguish.

He had been snatched from her almost as soon as he was given. She knew deep down it was for the best, but why not before he had drawn his first breath of life and saved him all that pain?

"God bless you my angel. Join your sister in Heaven," she whispered as she laid him to rest.

A FRESH START

Ruth visited a solicitor during the next few weeks with the intention of filing for divorce. He was an elderly man with a kind face, and was convinced that she had just cause for the divorce to proceed without much trouble on the grounds of adultery.

Ruth's nerves were playing her up very badly at the time and she cried at the least little thing. Harry was still living at home, but only for limited hours during the night in the spare room, leaving his washing and giving Ruth some money for the bills. He was rarely home for meals, so seldom saw the children for days on end. The situation was almost impossible to bear. He was still going out in the evenings until the early hours of the morning.

Ruth was coping as well as she could with the girls. The doctor had put her on Librium and Valium tablets to help her with the shaking sessions she was experiencing. She was finding the side effects very disturbing, however, as she fell asleep quite easily if she sat down too long. Also she was having trouble remembering what she was doing half the time. One day she found herself in the town and could not remember getting there, or what she had done with her girls. She urgently rang Mags to hear the girls were all right; they were at school and nursery. On returning home, Ruth flushed the tablets down the toilet and made her mind up to be strong for the sake of her children.

She decided not to go through with the divorce. She felt she could not stand up in court and reveal personal details of their life together. She would give Harry one more chance to rectify what the problem was with their marriage; she would talk to him for the sake of their children.

Harry said there was no problem. It would be difficult for Ruth and Harry to become friends again, but they both agreed to try.

It took quite a long time on Ruth's part, as she had been so badly hurt by it all. Harry did try, so slowly he moved back into her life.

Marie was seven and Tracy was four and soon to start school. Whenever possible, they all visited Mary and Albert on a regular basis. Mary had been ill during Ruth's trouble so knew very little of the circumstances of Andrew's death.

It had been very hard for Ruth not to confide in Mary; it would have helped her a great deal in her own distress. They were very close to each other, even closer than Ruth and her own sister. They had shared most of their troubles together, and Ruth felt so alone with her burden without her dear friend to talk to.

Mary had actually had a nervous breakdown. She had been admitted to the local psychiatric hospital as a voluntary patient during Ruth's troubles and did not know anything about Andrew or the trauma of his death. Albert had asked Ruth not to tell her, as Mary had to have no upsets whatsoever.

Mary by that time had two children, a boy and a girl. They were both attending school, being of similar age to Ruth's girls.

The sparkle had gone out of both their lives when at last Mary came back home. Slowly, they tried to cheer up together, pick up the pieces and put their lives back on track.

Mary told Ruth on one visit, that they were to move house into one that they were having built.

"Come with me, Ruth, to look at my new house," Mary asked one day on her usual visit. "We're having it built in the country away from the traffic. It's a little further for you to travel, but there's a regular bus service. It will be nice to hear the birds singing instead of car noises all day long."

"We'll go tomorrow afternoon if the weather is nice - I could do with some fresh air," Ruth replied with a smile. "I think Harry and I will be moving too. We've decided to buy our own house so that he can set up in business for himself. I'll tell you about it tomorrow when I see you. Bye for now, I'll see you around two o'clock."

"This is the stop," Mary said, after a bus ride lasting half an hour. "We just have a short walk away from the road, around the corner." With amazement showing on their faces they both started to laugh, for all there was to see was a great sea of mud with trenches dug everywhere where the sewers were to be laid. There were diggers everywhere with men up to their armpits with mud, grinning at the pair of them.

"It's lovely, Mary, your new house," Ruth teased. "We'd better go and look at mine – there's a little more of it to see." Together they left with red faces, but both giggling away.

The terrace of four houses was situated up at the top of a hill, the last block in the road, surrounded by open fields overlooking the town.

"We can't go in as the other people are still living there, but what do you think of it?" enquired Ruth of her very dear friend.

"I like it. It has a nice bay window overlooking the front garden, which is very pretty and well kept. You'll be able to see the sunsets over the town at night, and look - there are horses in the fields at the back. You'll be living here before mine is even built."

True to Mary's words, Ruth and Harry moved in before the end of the month.

"A fresh start," Ruth thought to herself. "Maybe we can forget some of the troubles we've been through together."

It was a nice house with two bedrooms, a beautiful blue bathroom and quite a large kitchen with a fitted gas fire. The bedrooms were large, both big enough to take double beds. The lounge was very pleasant with the bay window letting in the sunshine during the day. The neighbours were nice; the whole area was most pleasant. The girls were a ten minute walk away from school, which was surrounded by shops selling everything anyone could want, from fish to greengrocery; even a post office selling cards and gifts.

"I'm sure I can be happy here if Harry will only make the effort to be more of a home-lover and a good father to our girls," she told Mary on her first visit to her new home.

Eventually Mary also moved into her dream home and life began anew for the pair of them.

Alice had been left a legacy. Ruth felt happy for mum and her father. Alice had remained a friend despite Ruth's father and gradually they were able to forget the bitterness of the past. Ruth was always welcome at their house whenever she called. Alice was not in good health, so Ruth decided to clean for her two days a week while the girls were at school.

Out of their legacy, dad bought a car. They were going on holiday to Blackpool for a fortnight and Ruth persuaded mum to treat herself to some new clothes for the visit.

On the Friday, they all climbed into the new car to go to the town for their shopping expedition The weather was warm and sunny and a balmy breeze wafted by every now and then. On arrival back home, after a very successful day, Ruth took all the labels off the clothes and did the packing for them. She gave them both a hug, wished them bon voyage then took her leave.

Something was niggling at Ruth's mind during the evening. She had felt a little uneasy at her dad's driving and prayed they would not have an accident with the car. This feeling of uneasiness persisted most of the night.

At nine o'clock the following morning, Ruth heard a knock on the front door and opened it to find a policeman standing on the front step. Her heart missed a beat as she held her breath.

"I'm sorry, dear," he said, "but I have to inform you that your father has passed away."

That's what I had that uneasiness for, Ruth thought, *it was a premonition.*

The officer gave her no other details apart from the fact that her mother was at home alone. She set off as soon as she could to see mum and arrived to find Alice in a terrible state, with a face like a ghost, tear-stained, and red eyed. Putting her arms round Alice, she could feel her trembling.

"Oh love, what happened?" Ruth asked.

"We got up this morning at four but it was a bit misty, so dad said we should wait a bit 'til it cleared. He told me to make another cup of tea, then it might be OK to go. I did, but when I brought the tea back he was dead."

"I'm so sorry, mum, it must have been an awful shock for you. He must have had a massive heart attack." Ruth held her distraught mother in her arms. "I'll help you all I can to make the arrangements, mum. I'll have to cancel the hotel for you; it's a shame that you couldn't have your holiday first."

Ruth spent every day at her mum's after dropping the children off at school until she thought that she was strong enough again after the shock to cope alone. It had been quite a few weeks, and Ruth was beginning to feel the strain of coping with her normal duties of mother and wife.

"I must have a rest, mum," she told Alice one day. "I'll come every third day instead of each day, as I must get some work done at home. My washing is mounting and there are piles of ironing to do from the last wash. I haven't vacuumed for a while either."

Alice was not too pleased at the suggestion, but agreed nevertheless.

After catching up with her household chores, Ruth joined the Mothers' Union at the local church. Quite a few different events were being discussed there. Strawberry teas, mock auctions, play groups, jumble sales and such were in the pipeline. Other young mothers had joined forces to ease the burden a little of the older members doing such things as flower arranging in the church or cleaning the brass furnishings on the altar. The local vicar also wanted a volunteer for cleaning the church and the school hall after the playgroup had finished.

Ruth was that volunteer. She enjoyed working at the church; it was different to what she had experienced before and she had plenty of friends among the other mothers.

The money came in handy. Her time was spent between the church, her mum's house and her own home. She loved spending time arranging altar flowers, the church smelling nice after she had polished the pews.

The annual harvest festival had gone well. With the others, she had distributed gifts to the local pensioners. As the weather turned colder, pies and peas or fish and chip suppers were arranged. The jumble sales were hectic but very enjoyable, with all doing their best to make them a success.

Christmas was fast approaching; the school hall would need trimming for the nativity and the school carol service. Ruth was looking forward to it all for the first time since 1958.

At last she felt that she belonged to a community.

THE SEVENTIES

In came the Seventies, with Edward Heath as Prime Minister, whose Conservative government took the people through industrial chaos, power cuts, food shortages and the three-day week over the next four years.

An earthquake in Peru on May 31, 1970, killed 72,000 people and left another 700,000 homeless; the 'Asian flu' hit England and around 4000 died as a result of it; violence erupted in Northern Ireland; Henry Cooper won the European Heavyweight Championship; North Sea oil was discovered in the sea.

The Q.E.1 was destroyed by fire. V.A.T. arrived, purchases being either exempt, zero rated or having a charge of 10 per cent added; an absolute nightmare for retailers in the early stage. The result was confusion all around and paperwork galore.

The Queen opened the new London Bridge in 1973, the reason being that the oil tycoon, Robert McCullough, had purchased the old one for the sum of £1 million to take to Lake Havasu in America.

Around the same time, the Watergate Scandal made headline news around the world, resulting in President Nixon, who had been elected in 68, resigning on August 8, 1974, the first President in history to do so.

In 1974 the American forces left Vietnam, leaving tens of thousands of refugees homeless; desperate people taking to boats to escape the wrath of the communists with no hope whatsoever. The horror of Cambodia and the Communist regime of Pol Pot resulted in the deaths of 7 million people during 1975 and 1976.

At home in the UK a new terror known as Jack the Ripper was stalking the streets at night, named after his predecessor of the 1800s who killed in the streets of London. The pattern was the same: frenzied attacks on prostitutes and the horrendous mutilation of their bodies. The new Jack killed 13 women and attempted to kill another 7 around the country before being caught and sentenced in 1976 at the Old Bailey in London

The following year saw a happier time, with the Queen's Jubilee celebrations. People gathered together in happy spirits not seen since the end of the war. Everywhere was trimmed with red white and blue decorations. There was dancing in the streets and jubilee souvenirs were displayed in all the shop windows.

The British won   the tennis championship at Wimbledon; the first floppy discs were created for use in computers; the first test tube baby was born   in 1978, created by in vitro fertilization, and the hopes of childless families were raised to new heights by the process that became known worldwide as IVF.

Maggie Thatcher became the first woman Conservative Prime Minister in 1979, smiling broadly at the gathered populace as she learned of her election.

Princess Anne married Mark Phillips in a spectacular wedding shown on television. The princess looking beautiful in her wedding dress; a picture of happiness. Such remarkable things were happening in the world, many of which were previously unimaginable.

Ruth had her own event to celebrate. She had once more produced a child; this time a healthy son. Anthony had arrived with very little trouble after nine months of desperate worry for Ruth. He was a fine, healthy lad with fair hair and blue eyes, weighing in at seven and a half pounds.

After the birth the doctor suggested to Ruth that she considered sterilisation to avoid any further complicated pregnancies. Ruth eagerly agreed, knowing that then she would have to worry no more.

During the Seventies, more troubled times entered Ruth's life but the heartache she felt was not for herself but for her dear friend Mary.

After the birth of Anthony, Mary had also been blessed with a new son. The boy weighed a healthy six and a half pounds, but all was not well with Mary. She had a bout of postnatal depression which lasted for a number of months. Eventually she was admitted as a voluntary patient for treatment and complete rest at the local hospital.

On her return weeks later, she appeared to be back to her old self again and once more they shared laughter on each others' visits for a number of months. The boys were growing up nicely together, both toddling and talking, and many a happy hour was spent with the four of them together whilst the rest of the families were at school.

On one visit to Ruth's, Mary appeared to be confused and it seemed her old depression was returning. Ruth mentioned this to Albert when she next saw him alone, and he told her that Mary had not been very well due to her older teenage children giving her cause for concern and resulting in a great deal of anxiety.

On a number of subsequent visits, the tales Mary told Ruth seemed to be figments of her imagination. Ruth could not quite believe that they were true. Knowing that Mary had been mentally ill previously, Ruth dismissed these tales too easily.

On one of her usual visits to Mary's house, Ruth found her in a very distressed state. The police had been to visit Mary and questioned her about her elder son's activities. Some of Mary's clothes had been found at the local playing fields in the cricket pavilion and the police had become suspicious, thinking that someone had been molested or even killed.

It turned out that Mary's son took pleasure in dressing up in female clothing. He also liked to dabble in witchcraft, along with his sister, who to Ruth's dismay apparently had lesbian tendencies. No wonder Mary was out of her head with worry.

"What am I going to do with them?" asked Mary tearfully.

"I don't know, love; I've never encountered such things in my life before, and in fact I know very little about such situations," Ruth replied with a feeling of helplessness. This was her dearest friend and she felt so sad for her, but could offer no consolation.

Shortly after this episode Arthur told Ruth that he had enrolled the lad into the army to try and make a man of him. After doing his basic training, however, he was dismissed for stealing pay packets and given a dishonourable discharge.

Mary was now in a terrible state, and after visiting the doctor with her Albert had no alternative but to have her admitted to the local psychiatric hospital. Ruth took Mary's young baby home with her.

Harry was not too pleased with the baby's presence, but Ruth felt that Mary would have wanted her to care for her new baby son. Life was quite hectic, however, at the home of Ruth and Harry. Anne Marie was ten, so she helped as much as she was able, occasionally feeding the new baby whilst Ruth attended to Anthony.

Walks to the shops meant that Mary's baby and Anthony were laid at either end of the pram, which luckily was a large Wilson pram. There were two cots in the bedroom, two mouths to feed and endless nappies to wash. Trying to keep the tots asleep without waking each other was a work of art. Ruth loved every minute of it, but Harry was not too enthralled and it gave him an excuse to visit the pub more often than he had been doing, if he needed one. It seemed he was quickly slipping back into his old ways, much to Ruth's regret.

Mary spent a full twelve months in the hospital. Sometimes she came home for the weekend and returned on the Monday morning. During this time, relatives of Albert took it in turns to mind the baby and give Ruth a break.

When Mary at last was discharged, she seemed to be recovered. She did not mention the other members of her family at all and Ruth was very reluctant to refer to them in case it caused her any problems.

The two younger boys were then toddling and playing happily together in the garden. On one of Ruth's visits to Mary's, the children were as usual outside playing with their toys. The garden was well sealed off with a sturdy fence and it was safe to leave the children unaccompanied to use their imagination, with a watchful glance out of the window now and again.

Unbeknown to the two mothers, the children had managed to get into the unlocked garage. Ruth saw them there and went outside to get them out and shut the door, to be greeted by two turquoise-coloured tots.

"Mary, come here a minute," she called. "Come and look at these two rascals."

"Oh my goodness!" Mary exclaimed, "don't they look comical?" The children were laughing at their mothers with such funny turquoise faces. "It's a good job it's only emulsion paint and not gloss or we'd never be able to get them clean again. Albert was in a rush the other day and forgot to go back and put the lid on properly."

Mothers and children laughed together as they tried to clean the paint off their clothes and bodies. Both boys went in the bath and all their clothes were hastily put in the washer. It took quite a long time to get the boys clean again, but they had a great time together in the bath amid the bubbles. For weeks later traces of turquoise paint could still be seen on Anthony's shoes.

After that the garage door was kept firmly locked.

GREAT SADNESS

Mary had appeared better for some time and life carried on in a pleasant manner. She delighted in her new son, of whose early life she had missed so much while away. He was a lovable child with dark hair, the image of Mary. On occasion she still talked about the wild things her elder children had done, yet they did not seem to trouble her as they had before.

Ruth was hoping that this time she was cured, but it was not so.

Within a month, Mary began her ramblings again about the things that were happening at her home during the night while Albert was at work. Chairs arranged in a circle; smoke-filled rooms; strange things happening overnight while she slept; the noises she heard from below. Ruth despaired.

Alice rang Ruth one Monday lunchtime.

"Have you seen the local news today on the TV, Ruth?" she enquired.

"No mum, why?"

Alice sadly related the report she had seen on the TV.

"Mary is in the special hospital - something about them being attacked in their own home. Albert has been rushed to a specialist hospital in another town with serious head injuries. The worst news is that the baby is dead."

Ruth began to shake uncontrollably, tears falling down her shocked face.

"I'm sorry, mum, I can't talk now, but thanks for letting me know."

She put the phone down, made herself a strong cup of tea and sat down to think. She rang Harry at his work.

"Harry, can you come home please?" Ruth asked after telling him the sad news. He came almost immediately, to find Ruth shaking from head to toe in a state of shock.

"Get in the car, Ruth," he ordered. "We'll go to the hospital and find out what's happened. But first we'll call at the local and get you a double brandy to stop you from shaking so much."

On their arrival at the hospital, Ruth found to her dismay a policeman standing outside the door to the ward. He would not allow her admittance. He took her name and address and said she would be interviewed later that evening. They had to go home without seeing Mary or finding out any details as to what had happened.

The rest of the afternoon passed painfully slowly until the evening news came on the TV.

What Alice had told Ruth was correct; the screen showed Mary's house. The statement said a body had been found and two people injured, one seriously, after an incident during the morning. Ruth was shocked to hear that the police were questioning other members of the family. That meant the children, as far as Ruth was concerned.

"Dear God, Harry! What has happened, do you think?" she asked tearfully.

"I can't imagine," Harry said, taking his shocked and trembling wife into his arms.

Later that evening two police officers arrived to take a statement from Ruth.

"You've known this lady for a long number of years, we are led to believe from statements made to us by her next of kin. We would like to hear what you have to say about her, please."

Ruth told them about their friendship over the years, the close bond they had always had for each other, and also about being worried about Mary's state of health for the last eighteen months. Everything she said was written down.

"We have questioned her teenage children and are ready to release them today."

"Where are they going?" Ruth enquired, knowing that they would not be able to go home in the circumstances.

"The boy is going to stay with friends, but the girl would like to come here if that is alright with you," she was informed. "But they are to stay where they can be contacted if necessary."

"Of course she can stay here," Ruth replied. " I wouldn't want her to go anywhere else."

Mary's daughter moved in that evening. No one was allowed to go to the house so Ruth had to do the best she could to clothe the girl temporarily. Luckily they were both of the same size.

Each day Ruth hid the daily papers from the eyes of the children. She dare not let them see the terrible headlines: "HOUSE OF HORROR" stared out at her in large lettering and there were photographs of Mary's house on the front page.

It was imperative that the children must be protected from the terrible details of what had happened to their 'aunt' and her family until she could find a way of telling them that would be easy for them to accept, especially her young son Anthony. He would miss his playmate more than the others. The thoughts of how she was going to tell him that his mate was no more haunted her every waking moment.

A week passed, and Ruth was disturbed by the sound of the phone ringing early one morning. She took the call, to be told it was for Mary's daughter. Ruth stood beside the lass as she answered the phone. The girl's face showed no emotion as she calmly told Ruth the sad news that Albert had passed away.

"We have to go to the hospital as soon as we can. Will you come with me and my brother, aunty, please?"

Ruth was perturbed at the lack of feeling displayed by the pair of them, especially as her own heart was so very sad.

Mary was charged with murder on two counts, one for the child and the other for her husband. As soon as she was well enough, she was arrested and taken into custody. The following day she was taken miles away to a remand centre. Ruth so desperately wanted to talk to her, but her requests were always denied. She did, however, talk to Mary's solicitor. He was a kindly man and seemed to feel compassion for Mary. They became friends, and both were determined that Mary would receive a fair trial if at all possible.

Due to the state of Mary's health, she was detained in the hospital section at the remand centre, yet Ruth was still denied access to her as visiting was banned whilst awaiting trial. The first time she saw her was in the Magistrates' Court, where Ruth sat in the public gallery. The press were present, eagerly anticipating a scoop.

Mary looked like a small, pathetic child standing beside the large wardress in the dock. Ruth's heart went out to her as the charges were read out. Mary showed no emotion; just stared ahead as if in a trance. The case was adjourned to a further hearing, the date of which was set, and the courtroom emptied.

This went on agonisingly slowly, week after week, until the case was finally transferred to the Crown Court in a different town.

In the meantime, Mary's daughter had been allowed to move in with a friend of hers and she had kept no contact with Ruth.

The lad contacted her and told her that the police had given permission for them to return home, and they had also given Ruth permission to clean the house.

Harry accompanied Ruth on her first visit and Mary's son met them at the door with the key.

He casually placed the key in the lock and opened the door. They entered the kitchen together. Ruth stared in horror at the state of the place.

"Come and look round," the boy invited, but Ruth and Harry were both outside being violently sick.

"I have to go now," said the lad nonchalantly. "You can take the key with you when you go, as I have another."

With these parting words, he was gone. Ruth and Harry stared at each other in disbelief. This was the place where his family had been killed, yet the boy was treating the situation as though it were an everyday occurrence.

"Please Harry, go home," Ruth begged. "I feel I have to do this alone, if you don't mind."

"Ruth, are you sure you're up to this task?" Harry enquired.

"Yes," she replied through her tears. "I'll be alright now. I'll do this gradually, room by room."

After Harry left she sat on the floor and broke down.

The whole kitchen was covered in blood. The curtains were stained, the walls were covered; even the ceiling was splattered with blood. A frenzied attack had clearly been carried out in there.

Ruth wondered if this was the result of some macabre witchcraft ritual carried out by the two teenagers. Mary had often spoken about finding the rooms full of smoke and chairs standing in circles on a morning when she got up, but Ruth had always dismissed this sort of talk as the ramblings of Mary's troubled mind. Now, however, she had her doubts. Ruth's thoughts constantly went back to conversations she had with Mary on numerous occasions about the family's dabbling in witchcraft and she began to think differently.

Picking up some eggs from the floor, she noticed that they were still intact except for a slash across the middle as if a knife had been stuck in rapidly without breaking the rest of the shell. They had not been dropped there, either. Other things troubled her; she later discovered the family bible while searching in the attic for some rags. The bible had a large triangle cut out of all the pages.

A hand-written poem almost describing the horrific scene was discovered under the mattress on the bed in the son's room.

On entering the room Mary and Albert had shared, a feeling of nausea attacked her again at the scene before her. Here was the place Albert must have been sleeping after his night shift at the local mill, unaware that he would shortly be hospitalised with head injuries where a hammer had penetrated his skull, smashing it to pieces as he slept.

Ruth turned and ran away from the terrible sight of the blood-stained bed, unable to do any more that day. She wept uncontrollably as she ran down the street, shaking from head to toe, admitting to herself that she needed Harry to help her with that dreadful room.

The following morning Ruth made a phone call to the Council for an urgent collection to be made at Mary's house. She briefly explained the details of the collection she needed and the circumstances that led to the urgency of her request.

She took two pills to try and relieve her raging headache, the result of a sleepless night tossing and turning, her mind in turmoil.

Harry accompanied her to the house and into the bedroom. They rolled the bedclothes and mattress together before throwing them out of the window to the waiting Council men, who had turned up promptly in answer to her request. Next went the carpet and curtains before she got down to the task of scrubbing the floor and walls, Harry helping her with washing the ceiling.

Soon all evidence of what had happened in the room had been obliterated, yet the smell of blood remained in her nose. She went for a walk in the fresh air for a while before returning to start on the bathroom. That was not too bad except for lots of water on the floor, but then she found large clumps of hair behind the radiator still showing signs of skin attached.

Harry had stayed all day with her this time. Between them the work was soon done and the house made presentable. It would be alright now for the teenagers to move back in.

They never did.

After a few days Ruth visited the solicitor with the hand-written note and found that he was also quite perturbed by it. He told her that the baby had been drowned in the bath, hence the water on the floor, but no other marks had been found on him. Albert had died from a fractured skull and severe head injuries, causing him to suffer heart failure, the post mortem had revealed.

Mary had also suffered substantial head injuries and there were splinters in her skull from hammer blows. The police had put this down to her having inflicted the blows herself after discovering that the child was dead, in an attempt to end her own life along with his. When she had failed to do it, the police said, she must have run round the house in a frenzy, hitting her husband, her own blood spurting in all directions.

The trial day finally arrived. Ruth had been told to be present in case she was needed to be called for the defence.

Mary was led up to the dock, looking even smaller than the last time when she had appeared at the Magistrates' Court. The weight seemed to have dropped off her; she was much thinner. Her face was ashen, her head bowed and her eyes unfocused and heavily ringed by dark shadows. She appeared unaware of her surroundings.

The reporters were there, waiting like a pack of wolves for their prey. The barristers in their wigs took their places in the court and all stood for the entrance of the Judge in his flowing red robes, whereupon silence descended on the court.

Ruth began to pray silently, her heart pounding in her chest and her head throbbing.

"Please God, let this go well for Mary."

The charges were read out. The accused had allegedly drowned her son in the bath before killing her husband with hammer blows. The charge was murder due to the fact that she had left the house to collect the hammer from the garage, making it a premeditated act.

Mary's plea was guilty on the grounds of diminished responsibility.

The judge asked for the psychiatric reports to be read out. This was not possible, as the reports had been left at the remand home miles away, so the case was adjourned to enable them to be sent for. This only took a matter of hours, during which time Ruth wandered across the road to the nearest public house for some lunch.

She found Mary's son and daughter already sitting there eating. They made no attempt to join her, as they were sitting with their respective friends, but it seemed to Ruth that they were having a good time.

Did they not realise what could be the consequences of today's case? she asked herself, or was it that they really did not care at all? Ruth was appalled at their uncaring attitude but managed to control her temper and leave matters well alone, for she knew she would go too far if she began on the heartless pair.

The court was reconvened and the reporters, pens at the ready, took their places. The court officials entered, followed by the judge. A hush descended in the courtroom.

Mary was once more in the dock, but her family were not present this time. No details were given out about the deaths, only details of Mary's health problems. Ruth was not called as a defence witness at all; in fact there was no defence.

There was nothing about the antics of the teenagers or the stress they had caused Mary. Nothing was said at all about anything, making Ruth quite annoyed. All the court officials were bothered about was that Mary had had mental problems in the past, therefore in their opinion she was not of sound mind when these horrendous crimes had been committed.

The judge summed up. He sentenced Mary to four years in prison on the proviso that she be detained in the prison hospital section for her own sake, under supervision. He considered her no danger to anyone but herself.

The details of what had happened that fateful morning were never disclosed. Ruth could not help but wonder if the right person were standing there in the dock, facing four years in jail - perhaps others were responsible?

The trial was over.

On one of her many visits to the prison where Mary was being held, Ruth was told of the shock treatment she had undergone and the callous way the staff and her fellow prisoners treated her. She suffered verbal abuse day after day because she had been convicted of killing a child. She had also been in the hospital operating theatre to have the bone chips removed from her skull.

Her teenage children visited her very rarely, much to Ruth's annoyance - poor Mary was facing this terrible ordeal without their support.

Ruth did her best to bring a little light relief into Mary's world. During the spring she would take a bunch of daffodils from the garden, but was dismayed when they were taken from her at the desk. She was searched each visit and her handbag contents displayed for all to see. The daffodils had long stems when she brought them, but were no longer than two inches when they were given back to her.

They had been cut down in a search for drugs.

Each visit was accompanied by cat calls from the male prisoners looking out of their cells into the yard where the visitors had to walk to gain access to the wing. Guards stood at the large doors with fierce-looking Alsatian dogs chained to them.

Ruth was never allowed to give Mary a cuddle - there was to be no contact between them; the ever-watchful guards made sure of that. Visiting was by permit only and had to be applied for regularly, sometimes without success.

"I can't remember anything after taking the sleeping pills and getting in the bath with the baby in my arms to drown us both," Mary said. "I didn't want him to grow up like the other two, you see. I was taking him with me when I ended it all. I just couldn't stay under the water. The rest is just a black tunnel without an end in my mind. Why was it not to be? Now I have to live the rest of my life knowing that I killed my son and Albert. Please God, forgive me," Mary pleaded.

Mary never did remember, although her health had improved by the time she was released. She moved into a small flat in the town centre for a while, then left the district to live elsewhere and managed to get a small job in a tobacconist's shop. Ruth continued to visit her, but not as often as she would have liked. She had to catch a train to get there but her time was restricted by the school hours and the responsibilities of motherhood.

In the meantime, Mary's home had been emptied by her son and daughter and the house had been sold. They both inherited their father's insurance money, the house and its contents. Mary was not allowed to profit from her deeds. She did not see much of her son or daughter after that. Many years later, Mary was eventually successful in taking her own life and ending the interminable daily torment she had endured for so long.

Ruth was not sad; she was relieved that at last it was all over for her dearest friend.

Another chapter in Ruth's book of life was closed.

FAMILY

Elizabeth had by that time had a family of her own; two boys and a girl. Each time Elizabeth had a child, Ruth had one the following year.

Anthony was a young toddler when Elizabeth's husband visited Ruth in tears to tell her his wife had deserted him and their children, much to the anger and amazement of Ruth. When eventually Ruth calmed down she visited Elizabeth at her place of work to talk to her.

"Why have you left?" she asked. "How could you, after the way we were brought up? I would never leave my children, no matter what," she shouted at Elizabeth. And believe me, I've had good cause to leave Harry."

Ruth could not understand why her sister would even contemplate leaving the family. She had a nice husband, three lovely children, a decent home, no worries as far as she knew. Her husband had always been a good father, telling the children stories at bedtime and taking the family out quite often. He was not a drinker like Harry - he was always home on an evening, playing with the family. Everyone had seemed ideally happy. He idolised his wife and their children.

Elizabeth had found a new man to brighten her life, she said.

"I love him, so we're living together from now on."

"You are selfishly only thinking about yourself at the expense of your children's happiness," Ruth rebuked her. "I personally don't consider you to be a very good mother, and indeed I'm quite shocked at your attitude, Elizabeth. I am ashamed to call you my sister."

Elizabeth was unperturbed by Ruth's remarks. She did not care what Ruth thought on the subject, and said so in no uncertain terms. They parted in an unfriendly way.

Elizabeth's hubby did his best to care for the children during the week. A friendly, kind-hearted neighbour looked in to help get the children ready for school so that he could go to work each day. She also took them in on an evening after school until their father returned home. He had shortened his hours to enable him to stay home to get them out of bed and feed them their breakfasts.

Elizabeth sued for divorce on the grounds of unreasonable behaviour, with her husband cross-petitioning her on the grounds of desertion. The divorce was granted, and Elizabeth was allowed access rights for the time being until the custody hearing, to visit the family home and see the children. She was allowed to see them on Saturday one week and Sunday the following week.

Elizabeth did not always turn up on the allotted day, making life very difficult for both the children and their father, not to mention Ruth. None of them knew what to expect of her.

The health of the children was beginning to cause Ruth some concern. The older boy had always suffered bouts of asthma from being a young infant, but now it seemed to worsen day by day for no apparent reason. The girl was starting to lose her hair in great clumps, leaving her with bald patches on her scalp. Her nails were also starting to look peculiar. Ruth took both the children to the doctor, who diagnosed stress.

Ruth asked their father what he thought was so bad that the children were worrying about it, but found he was as perturbed as she was herself. On asking the children, Ruth discovered that they were being taken to the flat where Elizabeth was living with her lover. Not one of the three children liked to do this, yet she made them. She was virtually dragging them through the town each time.

Most of these discoveries came to light amid many tears after gentle questioning by Ruth.

Ruth was appalled at her sister's behaviour. Had she no feeling for her children - was she taking after her own father? He could also be heartless, as Ruth had learnt at her own expense many years previously.

When Ruth told the children's father what the doctor had said he applied to the court for custody of the children on grounds of their health.

He had to endure visits from welfare representatives who inspected their home, looked at the beds and peered in his cupboards to make sure he had plenty of food in store for them. They made enquiries of the neighbours to make sure he was not leaving the children alone at any time.

Everything must have met their strict standards, for he was granted custody and access was denied to Elizabeth until the children were old enough to make up their own minds.

Elizabeth was greatly angered by this decision, for she had expected that her husband would have to move out of the family home enabling her to return to bring up the children without him but with her lover.

She blamed Ruth for interfering in her life, which created bad feeling between them. Ruth was, however, unperturbed by this as she had the welfare of her sister's children very close to her heart. She had seen how upset the children had been and listened to their weeping as they fell asleep in her own home for the first few weeks night after night, the younger one calling for his mummy. She had cried for them at her sister's desertion.

Ruth's life had changed again.

Each weekend the children joined Ruth's own at her home and they spent all the school holidays with Ruth and her family, giving her six children to look after. They were pretty good on the whole, but at times Ruth found it very tiring.

Sometimes she would get cross, but the children never thought she was angry so she began a system of counting to three. If she had to say "three" they got a quick slap. This worked like a miracle, as the one slap they had had in the beginning was quite a stinging one and they soon learned that when she told them to do something she meant it.

Many a wet day was spent with numerous boxes and paper bags and a small pair of weighing scales from the pantry. Playing at shops was always a firm favourite, weighing out the rice, peas, lentils, flour and so on - a bit messy, but well worth the hassle of cleaning up afterwards. They played for hours together, each one being shopkeeper in their turn. Ruth amassed numerous boxes and tins to add to the shop; a bit of a nuisance to store, but nevertheless necessary for the game.

Wet and miserable days were sometimes spent having a baking session, making small biscuits and buns for tea enjoyed by everyone. Ruth often made them a 'Desperate Dan' pie, as she called it, from corned beef and onions and potatoes in a huge pie dish with a thick piecrust on the top. It was the best way to fill their ever-increasing appetites on a limited budget.

Dry days were spent either with a treasure trail prepared by Ruth before they arrived or a visit to the local park, which had a museum that the children loved to visit time and time again. There was an aviary with budgerigars and canaries flying freely around and peacocks strutting about calling in their loud voices, displaying their beautiful plumage.

The younger children held Ruth's hands on either side with the older ones holding each others' and they all marched together in a line. It must have been a comical sight, as Ruth was only five feet tall and the older boy was rapidly catching up on her in height.

Other days were spent catching a bus and walking to a nice spot to play with a football. Ruth would pack a picnic lunch for each child; a small bottle of pop and a few sweets were made into small parcels to be carried by each one of the children.

The only other requirement was sunshine, and away they would all go.

Happy Days.

EMPLOYMENT

Ruth's elder daughter was at secondary school, the younger one at juniors and her son was attending nursery school during the day, enabling Ruth to get on with her household chores and attend to Alice. One morning, she heard at her local shop about a vacancy at the local hospital, which was just around the corner from where she lived.

The job was for a nursing auxiliary, doing the evening shift of five hours: four o'clock until nine five evenings out of seven. The girls finished school at three thirty, enabling them to get home to look after their younger brother until their father came home at teatime. She would be able to see that they were alright before she left for work.

Harry promised to come home each evening instead of going to the pub, which had got to be his usual habit for far too long in Ruth's opinion. He also agreed that the extra money would come in handy.

Ruth's interview was a successful one; she was to start the following week. The vicar had given her an excellent reference, the matron told her.

"I'm sure you will make a very good member of our nursing staff and I hope you will be very happy here," she said.

It was to be a very happy experience for Ruth that lasted for eighteen years, but after the first evening she almost did not return for the following night's shift. To her dismay, Ruth had been assigned to a men's ward. The charge nurse had a wicked sense of humour, which Ruth found rather embarrassing.

Her first patient was of foreign origin, unable to understand a word of English. She was instructed to watch him and not let him leave the ward for any reason. He ran everywhere, jabbering away in his strange tongue fifty to the dozen. After a tirade of words, he promptly emptied his bladder all over Ruth's new uniform, to her absolute horror. This, however, greatly amused the charge nurse and his partner, who had expected the patient to do just that. It had been his usual way of greeting every new member of staff to the ward until they became used to him.

Two of the other patients in the day room decided to have a fight and empty flower vases over each other, fists flying in all directions. There was not too much damage, as both of them were well over eighty years of age. Most of the others joined in by shouting encouragement to one or the other of the men. It became very noisy at one point, with all of them shouting at the tops of their voices; verbal abuse the likes of which Ruth had never heard before.

Her partner was a Jamaican lady with an infectious laugh; a great bundle of fun at any time. She could, however, get the men to behave.

Ruth found the work very strenuous, as she was just over five feet tall. Trying to lift men twice her own size into bed, most of them unable to stand, undress or wash, took a lot of effort on her part.

She found the most embarrassing thing about it all was having to wash the men's private parts, which of course the men were delighted about. While she was attending to them, they constantly made lewd remarks which the charge nurse found hilarious, commenting along with the patients and making Ruth's face turn scarlet. At the end of her first shift she could not get out of the door fast enough.

She was sure she would not be attending the next evening.

But she did return, having thought about it all evening and well into the night. Ruth did not want to appear a defeatist, remembering the vicar's words when she had told him she was applying for the job.

"They are all long stay patients, Ruth, and they will spend the rest of their lives in the hospital. They're suffering from senile dementia or maybe strokes and are unable to look after themselves any more. You are far too soft hearted for a job like that," he had said. "It will be very hard for you to come to terms with death after knowing patients for a long while; most of them are elderly and very dependent on the nursing staff."

Ruth felt she had to prove him wrong, especially after the excellent reference he had given her.

All the patients in the hospital were in their eighties or nineties and quite a number of them were very confused, yet Ruth found the job so rewarding. Many a fond attachment was formed and Ruth treated the old people as though they were the grandparents she had never had. She loved them all. Her job varied from dressing, bathing and cleaning some poor soul who had not made it to the toilet in time to spoon feeding the more infirm, bed making and shaving.

Her elderly patients had such tales to tell of the bygone days of their youth. Some had even served in the First World War. One man in particular, who had eyes tattooed on his rear end, tormented Ruth each time she washed him as he could make one of the eyes appear to wink as he tensed his muscles.

During her time there she worked on all the wards in turn, which was hospital policy to avoid the nurses forming attachments to any patient in particular. This was hard, as there was usually a favourite patient on all the wards.

Tommy was one such patient for Ruth. He was a small man in his nineties, very thin, with a face no bigger than a child's. He rarely spoke to the nurses and always looked as if he was afraid, yet at times his eyes held a twinkle that Ruth found irresistible on the rare occasions that he smiled.

He had been in the Medical Corp during the war, serving in Italy. To Ruth's amazement he had stacks of photographs of his army days in his locker. He formed an attachment to Ruth, constantly following her around the ward. If he needed any help, it was always Ruth who he asked for assistance.

There was nothing she liked better than to sit with Tommy every spare minute and talk to him about his career in the army. He told her many tales of his experiences as a medic.

However, he developed a fixation in his head that Ruth was his wife. He hated her to go home at the end of her shift and often asked her the following day where she had spent the night. He often shouted at her in fluent Italian when he was cross with her, yet he couldn't understand why she could not answer back in Italian.

His small, shuffling feet followed her everywhere she went in the ward like a lost soul wandering in the desert, sometimes very near to tears when he could not understand the reason behind her answers at times.

The elderly ladies who had never married were also a delight to Ruth; they were so particular in their ways. Everything had to be just right and Ruth could tell that some of them had come from wealthy families. Ruth liked to attend to such ladies, as they were so appreciative of anything she did to make them more comfortable. If she had the time she would spend a little longer doing their hair and maybe putting on a little perfume for them. They would reward her with such a lovely smile that it made her heart glad.

Not all the staff, however, were so pleasant and many a time Ruth would have chastised them if she had been in a better position, yet she had to keep quiet. They were doing what they were paid to do, but without the care she felt was required of them and very little niceties were shown to their patients. Ruth felt that they were there just for the money, unlike herself who enjoyed the job and got such satisfaction from knowing she was doing what she thought the elderly patients in her care deserved.

On some wards the staff did show some compassion to their patients and strong attachments were made with such fellow carers which lasted for years.

Harry was not being fair to his family. Ruth found that many an evening his tea would be still in the oven when she returned from her evening shift and Anne Marie had put the younger children to bed without her father's supervision. He was slipping back into his old ways of visiting the pub straight from work. No matter how often she complained to him about it, Harry still persisted in doing it.

On numerous occasions he began to stay out longer, sometimes until four in the morning. His excuse was that he had been playing cards with his pals at their homes after closing time.

Ruth was also finding that he was not supplying her with the same amount of housekeeping money, and she was finding it very difficult to pay all that was necessary in the home. Harry seemed to be unperturbed by this.

The worst thing Ruth was to discover was lipstick on his collar after a 'card- playing' session.

Their relationship began to deteriorate rapidly. Harry did not care either for his children or Ruth, it seemed, as he went about his own business. Ruth's health began to suffer, the shaking started again and many a sleepless night was spent alone worrying. She began to lose weight, which made her job so much harder as she lacked the strength necessary to lift the patients.

One or two rumours were getting back to her about people seeing him in the pub with various women on a too-friendly basis. When she approached him on the subject he always denied it, but later he would start an argument and sometimes threatened her. He began to throw things around the house or storm out in a rage.

In the meantime, Ruth was trying to keep her job and also attend to her own children and at times her sister's children, who still came to her at the weekends and school holidays.

The strain of it all was rapidly telling on Ruth.

On a visit to her parents- in- law, Ruth was dismayed to find that they were siding with Harry. Where had she gone wrong? She had always tried to make a happy home life for them all. Had she perhaps spent too much time with the children, and was Harry jealous of that? Their sex life had not deteriorated at all, so that could not have been the problem.

Eventually, on advice from her work friend, she attended the Marriage Guidance Council but was told that Harry should have been with her. Ruth asked him to go but he refused.

"We're alright," he said, "we don't need them."

The situation got no better. Harry still insisted on carrying on his life the way he wanted, disregarding what Ruth thought on the matter.

One day at work, one of the staff asked her what was wrong.

"You look as though you're suffering from starvation, Ruth. You have to do something - you can't go on like this much longer. You'll be no good to yourself or the children if this situation doesn't alter."

Ruth agreed with her and began to search for somewhere else to live.

It was extremely difficult, as she had to consider the children and their schools, also the lack of money. She put her name down on the local council housing list but was told it was unlikely she would find a house as she was making herself voluntarily homeless.

Ruth explained to them about how her health was in danger with the worry, and how her responsibilities to her children made it imperative for her to get out of the situation she was in as soon as possible. A representative from the council called at her home to inspect it. They informed her that a flat was available with three bedrooms if she wanted it, since the situation was so urgent.

Together with a fellow workmate, Ruth went to have a look at the flat the following day while the children were at school. The condition of the flat was atrocious; it was very large and was in a block of four storeys. There was a very large room with a tiled fireplace. The kitchen contained a sink and drying cabinet running off a small hallway, and there was a staircase leading up to three bedrooms and a bathroom.

The walls and floors in the entrance to the flats were filthy; the staircase leading up to it was disgusting, littered with all sorts of rubbish. One of the bedrooms had animal faeces on the floor and scratches on all the doors.

The agent informed her that the previous tenants had kept rabbits and mice in the flat that was why they had been evicted.

"If you want it, we'll give you extra time to clean it," she was told.

Ruth looked around. Yes, it could be made into a nice flat with a lot of hard work and plenty of paint and wallpaper. She accepted it with an offer of help from her friend to clean it up.

Together they scrubbed and scoured it from top to bottom, cleaning away all traces of the previous owners and their animals. Twenty-four rolls of wallpaper were carefully put on the walls and lace curtains put at the windows, making it look more presentable day by day.

Outside there were four separate outhouses, one for each flat, stuffed to the ceiling with every obnoxious thing imaginable, such as soiled nappies and dirty cardboard boxes filled with pans full of stale food. Shoes and clothing, all filthy, mingled with the rest of the garbage on the floor. Flies were everywhere, buzzing around the foul-smelling contents of the outhouses. They were so full that none of the doors would shut.

"I will definitely have to have these cleaned out," thought Ruth, "I can't live near this mess at all."

The next day she went to the council and asked for it to be cleaned up.

"I work for the National Health," she told them, which was true really, but not in the way they took it.

Within days the whole area was cleaned and disinfected and new doors were fitted on each outhouse.

"That's better," she decided on inspection.

Ruth visited the shops and purchased a carpet for the front room, a cooker, a sofa and a gas fire all on hire purchase with her friend acting as guarantor for her.

"Goodness knows when I shall be able to clear this debt," she related to her friend after it had all been safely delivered to her flat.

The time of year was January and the weather was freezing when she arranged for the removal van to call at her home. Ruth had asked Harry for a divorce but he had laughed at her.

"Why do we want a divorce?" he had asked. "We're alright."

She was a little afraid of what his reaction would be on the final day, so asked the local police station if an officer could walk past the house at the time the van was there. Their answer was 'no.'

Unfortunately, the night before the day of departure, it snowed very heavily and Harry was late going to work. He had only just disappeared round the corner when the van arrived. It must have passed him on the road. Within minutes, a friend of Ruth's arrived with boxes, followed by another, also with boxes. Between them they packed the children's clothes and toys. Ruth grabbed her own clothing and a few sheets, bedding and towels. The lounge she left untouched, also the bedroom she had shared with Harry. She had to take the table and chairs out of the dining room and the children's beds. The rest of the home was left intact, even with Harry's tea prepared in the fridge for the evening and food in the cupboards.

The furniture van struggled up the snow-covered hill to the flat with great difficulty due to the state of the un-gritted roads. After everything had been unloaded, Ruth paid the cost of transit leaving her with just eleven pence to last them until she got her wage.

She set about putting the flat in order, making up the double bed the girls had shared before so that the three of them could sleep together. Anthony had a bedroom to himself next to theirs. Luckily the flat had built in wardrobes, which were a boon to Ruth. She could store all their things without having to buy extra furniture, which she could not afford.

Her friends left as she made her way to school to pick up Anthony and take him to his new home. He did not seem to bother about the move as long as his toys were there and he didn't ask about his father at all, much to Ruth's relief. The girls had been told previously about the move and each came to their new home as instructed.

After the children were in bed, Ruth sat alone without radio or TV, the hours dragging slowly by. The enormity of her situation began to dawn on her and the tears began to fall uncontrollably as she prepared to get into bed.

What have I done? Have I made the right decision? I have to bring this family of mine up alone now, as I cannot go back to that endless worry again.

Ruth spent a sleepless night tossing and turning between the girls, who used her as a kicking post all night in their sleep. *This won't do,* she thought to herself. *I shall have to sleep on the sofa in future.*

The following night and each night after that for a long time she slept there, covered in every coat she could find as she was short on bedding.

Social Services called to see if she was looking after the children properly. They decided that they had enough clothing between them, but she could qualify for free school meals. She was also allowed to purchase a bed for herself on the proviso that if the house she owned with her husband was sold the money would be paid back to them. Ruth gratefully accepted their offer. The children, however, had other ideas about the free school meals as they were being taunted by the other children about being poor.

Ruth stopped getting the vouchers and did her best to provide her children with a packed lunch each day.

She expected Harry to call on her at her work, but he did not. She did not know whether to be afraid of Harry or the Ripper (who had struck in her own town recently) as she made her way home at night along the dark path through the field to her flat.

Harry, however, did not bother her as he had moved in with his latest girlfriend, the latest of many he had had over the previous years, Ruth discovered much later after their divorce came through.

The visit Ruth had made to a solicitor following the death of Andrew was taken into account when she filed for divorce. She applied for maintenance for her children from Harry, but even though he was ordered by the court to pay he was most reluctant to do so and often missed paying it. This made it very difficult for Ruth, as she relied on the money to keep the family fed. Ruth worried that maybe Harry would apply for custody of the children to enable him to keep the house, but he did not attend or even have a solicitor present at the hearing, so custody was granted to Ruth in his absence. A few weeks later the divorce was granted.

The former marital home was still in dispute, however, as Ruth had informed the building society of her inability to pay the mortgage.

Harry did not pay either, so it was due to come up in court under a repossession order in the following months. Ruth hated where she was living; it was noisy and the neighbours were loud, foul-mouthed individuals who constantly had drunken parties, often lasting all night long.

She was concerned for her family when she was working on the evening shifts and worried constantly about her small son hearing all that commotion night after night, yet she could see no end to it.

Harry did not seem to be around anywhere but Ruth heard a tale that he had told at the local pub that she had gone off with someone and emptied the house, not even leaving him a teaspoon, therefore he had had no alternative but to move in with his girlfriend.

It made a great excuse for him.

CHANGES

Alice's health was beginning to deteriorate rapidly during the colder weather and her arthritis was much worse. She found it difficult to walk and was confined more and more to a wheelchair. Ruth arranged for the district nurses to attend her daily and she had the bungalow adapted to wheelchair use. A ramp was made outside the door, allowing Alice to go out on her own into the garden area to smell the flowers when the summer came. There was a lovely rose bed in front of her lounge window, cared for by the Council, so it was always in tiptop condition.

The sink, kitchen work surfaces and cooker were lowered to a height more suitable to a sitting position, enabling Alice to remain in the small place she called home. It was very cosy, with central heating. The bed had been moved into the lounge so that she could watch the TV from there if the nurse called early to put her there.

Everything seemed to work very well, enabling Ruth to carry on her shifts at the hospital and popping in to clean or shop for Alice when it was convenient for her between her household and children duties.

Ruth hated where she was living, so it made a pleasant change to visit Alice in nice surroundings. She did not go out anywhere else apart from the hospital, as she was afraid of meeting Harry with his new lover. She was afraid what her reaction would be if this happened.

She was finding things very difficult due to the shortage of money, which did not allow for anything other than food or bills, but Ruth did her best to keep cheerful in front of the children. Once they were in bed, however, the enormity of her situation would rear its head.

Anne Marie, who had grown into a delightful daughter in Ruth's opinion, had bought a certain record that was in the top twenty at the time and she played it constantly when Ruth seemed to be downhearted. It was appropriately named 'I Will Survive.' In the end both Ruth and Anne Marie laughed at the number of times she played it, yet it certainly did the trick. Ruth began to believe she could and would survive without Harry. The song became a favourite of Ruth's for many years thereafter.

Two months had passed since Ruth had left the family home, yet still no settlement had been reached about the divorce or the custody of the children. Also, the mortgage on the marital home was getting further and further into arrears with neither her nor Harry living there.

The pressure of worries was beginning to tell once more on Ruth, when a couple of her workmates decided she needed a night out. Anne Marie was old enough to look after Anthony so Ruth thought *why not?* The girls had asked her before but Ruth had always declined their invitations, as she knew she could not afford to accompany them.

This time, however, she did.

It was after a late shift at the hospital when all three of them had worked together.

"We'll go to the club tonight," they told Ruth. "It won't cost you too much there, as we're both members."

Ruth tidied herself up a little in the bathroom of the hospital after her shift, combing her hair and putting on a little make up and perfume.

"Are you ready, then?" the girls called to her. "We should go for the bus now, Ruth."

Taking one last look in the mirror, Ruth left the ward.

The club was a Singles Club, much to Ruth's dismay; she was certainly not looking for a partner. On entry she was pounced on by the organisers for proof of divorce or separation. Luckily she had some; a letter from her solicitor was in her handbag.

It had been raining rather heavily on their journey from work, so each had a soggy umbrella dripping on the floor as they crossed to the cloakroom.

Ruth was following the other two, and much to her embarrassment she almost did the splits in the centre of the wet dance floor. She was extremely reluctant to leave the cloakroom, knowing that everyone in the room had seen her trying to keep her balance. Since her trouble with Harry she had lost a lot of her confidence and self-esteem.

When eventually she did reappear, the other two were on the dance floor and obviously enjoying themselves. She sat on the nearest seat available away from the throng of men, who all seemed to her to be ogling at the women. *I really wish I hadn't come here,* Ruth thought to herself, *if only the floor would open and I could disappear.*

The music stopped and her friends joined her for a drink.

"What will you have, Ruth?"

"I'll have a bitter lemon please," she replied, not wanting anything intoxicating as she had not eaten much at teatime, and because she wanted to keep her wits about her in this place.

Her friend returned with the drinks, but before they had time to drink any the music started again. A voice announced a barn dance and away the two of them went on to the dance floor, leaving her alone again.

The organisers approached her with the latest newsletter for the club. Ruth was glad, as she could read it instead of getting involved talking with anyone. They told her that they had regular membership and met most weeks to allow single people to make friends, some meeting their life long partners in the process.

Ruth knew she would not be coming again after that one visit.

After they left her to attend to their duties, she sat reading the newsletter. She was occasionally being approached for a dance but politely refused, saying she wanted to read.

The music stopped again and to Ruth's horror the disc jockey announced that everyone on the floor had to get someone from the seats as a new partner.

This time she could not refuse, as all the people present were on the dance floor. The music started again, but then an announcement was made that the dance was to be a progressive dance.

"Each time the music stops you have to change partners."

There was no way out of that, but it was a good idea to get everyone dancing with each other.

Ruth joined in rather reluctantly, each of her partners asking the same questions time and time again.

"How long have you been divorced? How many children have you? Where do you live?"

She answered each time that her divorce was not through and that she had three children, two of whom were teenagers, and that she lived in the area.

One man asked her her children's names.

"Anne Marie, Tracy and Anthony," she replied.

"Where does Anne Marie work?" he enquired. She replied that Anne Marie worked for a solicitor.

"I think she knows me," he said, much to her surprise. "Has she got a friend called Jane?"

"Yes, they've been friends for a number of years," Ruth replied.

"Then I know who you are,"answered her dance partner.

Joe introduced himself.

"Jane is my stepdaughter and I've seen Anne Marie on numerous occasions. The solicitor where she works has been handling my divorce. It's by mutual agreement, as we can't get along somehow, due to us both being fiery-tempered."

Joe had been a regular in the army since he was a boy and still worked for the Ministry of Defence at the local drill hall as a civilian employee. He was also a serving member of the Territorial Army. He had been living on his own since his marriage had broken up. He was a regular visitor at the dance hall further along the road and asked if she would like to go there for a drink so they could talk without too many interruptions.

Ruth said goodnight to her friends, who by that time were really enjoying themselves in the company of two men. She was sure she would not be missed.

It was only a short distance to the dance hall and she went with Joe to the bar. The barmaid knew him and said a pleasant 'hello' to Ruth.

Joe told Ruth he had a bad temper and was not really a very nice person, yet a few of his fellow soldiers came to the bar and they genuinely appeared to like him, which contradicted what he said about himself.

Anne Marie had mentioned him to her many times as Jane's father, but had never said anything against him.

"You're not drinking bitter lemon all night - what about something stronger this time?" Joe asked as they sat down.

"I'll have a Bacardi and coke then, if that's alright with you please," Ruth said. "I usually drink that."

After a few drinks Ruth began to relax with Joe. He leaned over her and gave her a kiss, and to Ruth's amazement she enjoyed it. It seemed a long time since she had been shown any affection and she was quite vulnerable. Joe had an incredibly soft and gentle touch as he took her into his arms.

When the dance hall was closing, Joe invited her to his flat at the other end of the block, just two minutes walk away, to phone for a taxi. The flat was very tidy - unusually so for a man, Ruth thought. He told her it had been a doctor's surgery at one time. It had all the amenities required for a person living alone.

"Would you like a cup of tea before I phone for a taxi?" Joe asked.

"Yes please," Ruth replied without hesitation.

She was unaware of Joe's intentions, but whether they were good or bad she really wanted a cup of tea. She was such a trusting soul with no thoughts of any impropriety at all. The need to be wanted and loved was so great within her that she fell easy prey to Joe's advances. Together they made love, and it was an enjoyable experience for Ruth. Joe's tender touch and pleasant manner made it all happen so easily.

Ruth went home in a taxi to her children with a tiny spark once more alive in her life.

The following week it was Easter. Joe asked her to call him at the drill hall where he would be until lunchtime on the Thursday before leaving early for the Easter break.

Ruth also had to call Anne Marie for something at her work, but she got the timing wrong. She was angry with herself, thinking that it would be the last she heard from Joe as he'd think she wasn't interested if she hadn't called.

Joe, however, had other ideas.

He was not going to let her get away that easily.

NEW DAYS

Joe turned up on Ruth's doorstep complete with land rover and in army clothes, much to Anthony's delight: a real live soldier at his home. Ruth apologised for not ringing and explained that she had got the timing wrong. Joe forgave her. Ruth was pleased that he had called - perhaps he really was genuinely interested in her.

Joe told her about himself and his army life. He had been married twice before but neither marriage had lasted over seven years, probably due to his army commitments.

Ruth was a little despondent at this news but gave him the benefit of the doubt, as he appeared to be a caring, thoughtful man who treated her with courtesy and always opened doors for her to go through. This had never happened with Harry.

She was impressed, and their romance blossomed. Her children took to him easily. He introduced her to his work colleagues and she visited the sergeants' mess on numerous occasions as his guest. She seemed to fit in very well with the army way of life.

Her social life certainly improved rapidly. The events they attended were quite spectacular, with huge 'dinner dance' functions on a regular basis. Ruth began to sew herself some nice new evening dresses, something she had never worn before. Joe looked splendid in his Regimental mess uniform, consisting of a scarlet jacket and black trousers tailored to perfection. A white dress shirt, bow tie and scarlet cummerbund completed the outfit. A set of miniature medals he had earned during his service was proudly added to his chest, completing the whole picture of splendour.

The huge drill hall entrance was filled with flowers of every description, arranged artistically each side of the walkway. The main section of the hall was transformed with parachute silk that adorned the walls and ceiling, turning the whole place into a giant, multicoloured tent. A stage was decked out with plants and flowers where the live band played dance music.

The floor was polished to a high gloss, making it a delight to behold. The tables displayed regimental silver, the likes of which Ruth's eyes had never seen before.

Ruth eagerly awaited each new event. The ladies attending these events were a little disappointed with Joe, as he was an excellent dancer. Their own husbands, however, were quite content to stand at the bar relating to each other some army gossip. Joe had always made a point of asking each of the ladies for a dance on previous occasions.

Ruth could dance, but had not had much opportunity to do so with Harry as he always said he did not know how to. Ruth found this hard to believe as he had spent many an evening out at the local dance hall without her. It was lovely to be able to dance with Joe on the pristine dance floor at the drill hall and she loved every minute of it, sometimes spending half the evening dancing, much to the annoyance of the other ladies.

Together they twirled to the quickstep, which was always her favourite dance, spinning round the floor. The faster it went, the better Ruth liked it. Joe tried to confuse her but she always managed to keep up with him, laughing all the time at his artistic footwork.

Slow foxtrots were performed with grace and elegance, as were the waltzes. Joe's fellow soldiers nicknamed them Fred Astaire and Ginger Rogers. Many happy hours were spent on the dance floor together, the live band making it all complete.

Joe had gone away for a few days to camp when, much to Ruth's surprise, he phoned her at her work to say he would be home later in the evening for one night. The visit was not planned, but one of the officers had to come back to the town for some business and had asked Joe if he wanted to accompany him. Joe had said yes, as it gave him an opportunity to have a night out with Ruth.

"I'll meet you at the local after your shift," he said. "About nine, Ok?"

"Yes," replied Ruth, "but I will not have eaten."

"Don't worry about that - we can go for a meal," replied Joe.

Ruth was a fan of Demis Roussos at the time, so Joe took her to a Greek restaurant for their meal and asked for the music to be played. He ordered wine to accompany the meal; something Ruth was not accustomed too. The meal was delicious and the wine went to her head. The music created a very romantic atmosphere.

Joe took hold of her hand.

"Will you marry me?" he asked.

"Yes," said Ruth. It was so romantic.

When it was time to pay the bill, the waiter laid it on the table and Joe picked it up and felt for his wallet. It was not there. With great embarrassment, he told Ruth he must have left it at the barracks in his other jacket. He had got ready in such a rush that he had forgotten to put it in another pocket when he changed his clothes.

Ruth luckily had enough money on her for them to raise the full amount for the bill, although she had a mental picture of having to wash the dishes.

They laughed about it when they got outside, but decided that they would now have to walk home as neither of them had any money left for a taxi. They had just begun to walk the shortest way home when they bumped into a group of his young soldiers going to the nightclub. Joe asked them for a loan, which was readily granted, so they had their taxi money after all. A beautiful evening was complete.

Happy days.

Harry decided that he wanted Ruth back, so he paid her a visit.

"You can come back under your own terms. I'll agree to anything, if you will forgive me and come back home Ruth, please," he pleaded.

"No, Harry, you're too late. I've got myself together again and I have a new gentleman friend. I'm finally seeing sense for the first time since I don't know when. You can't hurt me any more. I'm looking forward to a much better life than the one I had with you for those last few years. You've killed any feelings I had for you. I was very hurt at first, then angry after all we'd been through together, although we weren't really together. I feel that I've carried a great burden alone for a long time, and now nothing about you appeals to me. I'm sorry for you, but it was all your own doing. We were married for twenty-two years, but now it's over."

Harry left without another word.

The romance between Joe and Ruth progressed happily.

He was kind and attentive to Ruth and her family, but sometimes a little strict with Anthony. Their home life, however, was improving. Joe bought Ruth a washing machine, which made her work load much lighter. He still lived at his own flat but spent a lot of time with Ruth at her home after meeting her from work when she was on the late shift.

He was away a few times at the weekends on army training sessions, as he was the drill sergeant putting the young recruits through their basic training.

Ruth's divorce came through, with Harry having to pay the costs. The custody hearing of the family was to be the following week. Ruth attended with apprehension. Her worries were unfounded, as Harry had sworn a declaration to the effect that he did not want custody, leaving the option open to Ruth. She was greatly relieved at this news.

Just the house problem remained, but it was to be a few weeks before a decision could be made regarding this.

Ruth had to be content living in the flat she hated, especially whilst passing her own comfortable home each time she went on the bus to town. Harry had not lived there at all since the day she left, the neighbours informed her when she saw them in the town. There was nothing she could do but wait for the court's decision.

She hated to see the litter and disgraceful, wanton destruction of the flats around her own. Graffiti was scrawled on the walls everywhere she looked. She was afraid of the influence it would have on young Anthony - he was only seven years old; a very impressionable age.

The other residents used bad language quite freely in every day talk and it was enough to make her ears curl. She hated to hear it and sheltered Anthony from it as much as she could. Joe spoke nicely, so maybe his influence would help.

The family readily accepted Joe's presence in their home. He began to stay over one or two nights after an evening out with Ruth. All was well until Tracy unexpectedly discovered him in bed with Ruth one morning, and ran out of the flat shouting at the top of her voice, "my mother is a whore."

Ruth was shocked at her outburst. She tried to explain to Tracy that eventually Joe would be living there permanently, so it made no difference now.

Joe was still keeping his flat going but they both thought it pointless to pay rent on two different places. Joe's flat was obviously not big enough for them all, so he would have to move in with Ruth.

The wedding had been arranged at the local Registry office. The vicar at Ruth's church had been told and he tried to persuade them to let him apply for special permission to his superiors to allow him to perform the wedding at his church.

Ruth told him not to bother but asked if he would bless their union in the church, to which he readily agreed. The wedding was set for September 22.

Ruth began to scour the town for her wedding outfit and for bridesmaid's dresses for the girls. Anthony was to act as pageboy. Ruth's searches were unsuccessful, as most of the wedding dresses were far too fancy for her age. Joe had said that he would be wearing his army dress blues, so Ruth wanted something on the classical side in cream. After repeated attempts, she decided to make her own and the girls' dresses.

Together they went shopping yet again, this time for the material required. Ruth chose a cream crepe material for her own dress with guipure lace as a trim. For the girls she chose a beautiful shade of turquoise nylon. Anthony was to wear a white shirt with a blue velvet bow tie and navy corduroy trousers.

The next thing they needed was patterns. Both girls were to wear long dresses with a small amount of trimming. After visiting numerous shops she managed to get just what she was looking for. All the dress patterns were in the empire line style. They all went home happy to have achieved their task.

Ruth spent many a night cutting out and tacking the dresses together, to be tried on when the girls had time between their other duties. She left her own dress until the last, as it needed more attention.

The final two weeks arrived. Joe was away at camp, giving her a chance to concentrate on her dress without him seeing it. Ruth got the basis sewn together, then started the time-consuming task of sewing on the guipure lace and tiny pearl buttons. She had made a detachable train to fasten on the back at the waist, so that she could maybe wear the dress without it at some army function at a later date. Her headdress and short veil also had to be made.

Between all this she was still attending to Alice, going to her job at the hospital and also doing her housework. It was all so hectic.

A friend at work had said she would make her the two-tiered wedding cake. The invitations needed to be sent out to their mutual friends.

Since Ruth had left Harry, she had had no contact with his side of the family; it was as if she had disappeared from the face of the earth. She was quite upset by this as her children no longer saw their aunts or grandparents, nor did they receive birthday cards from them.

It was no good sending invitations to them.

When she married Joe the children would gain new aunts and uncles, but unfortunately no grandparents.

Ruth's work friends were all invited and Joe invited some of his army friends. There should have been an exercise on the week of the wedding, so they would not all have been able to attend but for the intervention of the Regimental Sergeant Major. He promptly cancelled the weekend, making it possible for all to go to the wedding.

When the big day arrived Ruth woke early to find the sun shining through the window.

"Come on, girls, today is the day," she called happily. "It's my wedding day and the sun is shining to show its approval."

Both her daughters looked delightful and her small son very smart. They were all happy for her as she dressed herself, ready to go.

Joe was waiting for her when she stepped out of the car, looking so spectacular that he almost took her breath away. He was wearing his dress blues as he had said he would. A red sash crossed over his chest and his red and gold sergeant's stripes and the polished buttons on his jacket shone in the sun. The epaulettes on his jacket were piped in red and his trousers had a red stripe down the side. To complete the outfit he wore a peaked hat, also trimmed with red, with the regimental badge displayed on the front. Around his waist he wore a white belt. He certainly looked very smart indeed.

Ruth wore her homemade dress, but she was very pleased with the end result. The train hung just right and the material had not creased as she had sat in the car on her journey.

In her hands she carried a small bouquet of peach roses with white stephanotis and fern in the shape of a triangle, looking a picture against the cream of the dress. A delicate headdress of cream silk flowers with a short veil lay softly on her head.

The girls wore circles of delicate white flowers on their heads and carried white bibles, each decorated with a white satin ribbon and a peach coloured flower.

Ruth and Joe made their promises to each other, signed the register and then jumped into a car bedecked with white ribbons to go to the church for the blessing. The other guests followed behind.

On their arrival they waited until all the guests had entered the church along with Joe before Ruth made her entrance. As she approached the door with her son and daughters the wedding march began to play, much to her surprise, as she had not asked for it. On entering, she was amazed to see the church full, every pew with someone sitting in it. It seemed to her that the whole regiment was attending her wedding.

To complete the picture, the smell of fresh fruit and flowers greeted her. Everything looked so beautiful, the church ablaze with colour. Ruth had not known but it had been the Harvest Festival on the Sunday so the church had been prepared in advance for her benefit, thanks to the young mothers' group, who also were in attendance.

What a difference this wedding was compared to when she had married Harry. Surely this marriage to Joe, with the church blessing, would turn out much better than the last one. After the photographs had been taken, which took quite a while, the newlyweds and their guests were taken to the drill hall for their champagne reception in the sergeants' mess, all arranged by Joe, unbeknown to Ruth.

During the afternoon Ruth made a point of visiting the hospital where she worked with her new husband, her son and daughters. She had promised the patients that she would go and was very pleased that she had when she saw their faces, especially the ladies. Gasps of delight echoed around the ward.

They returned to the mess for the speech-making and the toast to their future happiness.

A good time was had by all, especially young Anthony who had been trying the champagne whilst Ruth and Joe were talking. He was quite merry when Ruth noticed him. After people began to disperse, Ruth and Joe took him home to bed.

In the evening there had been a disco in the large drill hall on the magnificent dance floor followed by a buffet supper. More guests had been invited to the evening event, including the hospital staff she had seen working during the afternoon on her visit. All had promised to come in the evening.

After a short sleep, Anthony had recovered sufficiently to attend the disco. He danced his little feet off all night, thoroughly enjoying himself along with everyone else.

Mountains of presents were brought for the happy pair, with enough drinking glasses to furnish a bar, all different types and colours. Clocks of every description arrived: kitchen clocks, travel clocks and so on - an abundance or clocks. They laughed each time they opened a new parcel.

The day ended at last and they went to their home together. Ruth had a new name and a new husband.

A new life.

A FRESH START

There was no honeymoon due to family and work commitments; it was impossible to find the time. Ruth settled down with Joe in permanent residence and life carried on much the same, yet a little happier than previously as now she had no money worries.

Anne Marie had moved out of their home to live in a flat with a colleague, leaving Tracy, who was courting strong, and young Anthony, who was still at school, living with Joe and Ruth in the flat.

Ruth's own home came under review with the court and she received a letter from the building society about the repossession. She dearly wanted to go back to it, as the area she was in was getting worse by the day. The day finally arrived when the situation was to be resolved.

Joe accompanied her to the court. Her heart was pounding as she entered the courtroom. *What will be the outcome?* she wondered, *will my home be mine or not?* Harry was standing to the side of the room staring straight ahead of him. He was unaccompanied by his solicitor, so the case was thrown out yet again.

Was he doing it deliberately, Ruth wondered or was there some other reason for it? As she left with Joe, she was to find out what Harry had in mind. He caught up with them and asked if he could speak to Ruth in private.

"If you pay the arrears on the mortgage, you can buy me out of the house for a certain amount," he said. Ruth was a little wary of his suggestion but still desperately wanted to go home.

"The remaining mortgage owing on the house is £6000. I'll settle for half that amount, then it will be yours for the duration," he informed her.

"I want that suggestion putting in writing through your solicitor please, then I may consider it," Ruth replied.

Harry nodded, then walked away without another word.

Ruth discussed the proposition with Joe and between them they decided they would go through with it if possible. It depended on the building society's approval of a loan in their joint names, which meant Ruth had to virtually buy her own house again.

The wheels were set in motion before she received Harry's offer from his solicitor and it was only a matter of weeks before the sale was finally agreed and they could move house.

Joe cancelled the tenancy of his flat, bringing with him lots of household goods. Ruth had also bought more necessities when she had moved to her flat, so they now had three of many things. Besides the abundance of houseware, they also had all the wedding presents.

They managed to dispose of the extra three-piece suite and some of the other surplus goods to Ruth's niece, who was getting married.

It felt great to be home in her own house once more. Ruth began to feel settled. Now perhaps she could put back on some of the weight she had lost with all the worry of the previous tribulations.

Alice was pleased for Ruth. She had worried about her, although her own health was deteriorating rapidly and Ruth arranged for the district nurses to attend Alice more often. Ruth's shifts had been altered at the hospital, making it more difficult for her to attend to Alice as often as she would have liked.

Elizabeth began to visit Alice during the day, but never when Ruth was there. She took over the responsibility of collecting Alice's pension, much against Ruth's wishes. It gave Elizabeth a good excuse to keep track of what her own family were doing, as they often visited their grandma.

Ruth continued doing the housework for some time, then applied for a home help for Alice. She turned out to be a very pleasant lady who Alice took to straight away, much to Ruth's relief.

Joe was finding it very hard to settle in Ruth's old marital home, feeling that it still belonged to Harry. He mentioned this to Ruth, who was fearful of what he wanted to do about it.

They discussed it and decided to try and find some other place that they could buy together and replace the furniture, so the house went up for sale and Ruth tried the agents' offices for a suitable property. After a few disappointments with various properties, she found a bungalow in a secluded cul-de-sac. It was in a pretty corner and had a Georgian bay window at the front. As soon as she saw it from the end of the road, she knew that it was what she wanted.

On entering double gates up the concrete drive to the side door, she came across a gigantic garden. It had been sadly neglected for some time but had originally been very well planned. She could picture it in her mind's eye, back in its original beautiful state. It had a greenhouse and a garden shed, as well as a vegetable plot. It would take a lot of hard work to bring it back to its former glory but she was willing to give it a go.

The agent had told her that the previous tenant had lived in it since it was first built, but unfortunately he had died. His relatives lived abroad in Australia, except for his nephews who lived in another town. The bungalow had been occupied illegally by squatters in the meantime and was badly in need of repair. Ruth did not mind as she had fallen in love with it.

Her own house sold almost immediately and she informed the owner of the bungalow. They immediately took the bungalow off the market, giving her a key to enable her and Joe to get someone in to do the repairs.

The builder gave them a quote for a new bathroom and kitchen, patio doors, new window frames where the doors had been, rewiring, building a stone fireplace and fitting a living flame gas fire. There was also a problem with water in the foundations, some of it due to a faulty water pipe, but also due to land drainage. The builder was to pipe the ground under the bungalow and fit a sump. The joists had to be treated with damp proofing and one or two of them needed replacing. The small bedroom and the bathroom needed new floor boards. The building society wanted all this work doing before granting them a mortgage.

The cost of all the work came to three thousand pounds. It was a great gamble, but they took it. The sale of the house appeared to be straightforward so they had some money to put down as a deposit on some new furniture for the bungalow.

Tracy was getting married and she was in the process of buying her own house, so she would be glad of their surplus furnishings. This was agreed between them all.

The bungalow had its work completed, the mortgage was granted and half the new furniture had been delivered. The removal date had been fixed.

Joe and Ruth were living with very little furniture, due to the majority of it having been moved to Tracy's. The floors were without carpets and the staircase grippers snatched at their feet each time they walked up the stairs. They were sitting on bean bags on the floor and eating off their knees.

Disaster struck!!

The first person in the chain involved with the sale of Ruth's house was made redundant and gave back word on the first sale.

Ruth could not believe this could happen; everything else was in place. The whole chain collapsed, each one giving back-word until it got to Ruth and Joe.

"Oh my goodness, what shall we do?" she asked Joe. "We owe all that money and now maybe we cannot pay it."

Joe came to the rescue. He had a young WRAC at the drill hall wanting a house. He told her about it and she decided to buy. Now they could all proceed as planned.

It was a great relief for Ruth, and everyone else concerned.

The dates were changed slightly, but in the end the day for completion throughout the chain arrived. The money had been transferred, and at last they could move into their bungalow.

It felt just right with all the new things about them; everything chosen together.

A fresh start.

REVENGE

The district nurses and Ruth were still attending to Alice when she took a turn for the worse. The nurses unfortunately did not notify Ruth, but instead contacted Elizabeth. Ruth was not due to visit mum for two days because it was almost Christmas: the staff were working extra hours and there was an alteration to her normal shift pattern.

It was quite a pleasant time to be on the wards, as they regularly had choirs from the local churches singing carols for the patients in the evening. Other days, schoolchildren would attend with their own versions of carols, which most of the patients loved and sometimes sang along with them.

The wards had to be prepared for the Christmas festivities. There were trees to be trimmed, wards to be decorated with Christmas garlands and cards to be written. Every patient received new clothes to wear for Christmas day and all these had to be sorted into sizes for everyone and labelled with their names.

There were numerous concerts arranged for the entertainment of patients and staff in the social hall, which was across the garden area. This meant extra work, wheeling the wheelchairs back and forth to and from the wards. It was very tiring, but pleasurable and quite a change from the normal routine of hospital life.

Ruth returned home one particular evening, tired but very pleased with how the concert had turned out.

The phone rang and Joe answered it. It was Anne Marie, informing him that she had some bad news for her mother. She had received a call from her cousin, Elizabeth's daughter, to say that her brother had asked her how Ruth was following her sad news about Grandma.

Anne Marie had been unaware of any bad news, so asked for details and was told that her grandma had died two days previously. She knew that Ruth did not know, so asked Joe to break the news to her gently.

Ruth was stunned, because she had expected to be informed of any deterioration in mum's health by the district nurses. What was Elizabeth thinking of to hide information like that from her?

When Ruth had time to collect herself, she phoned Elizabeth, who told her that she did not want to speak to her and slammed down the phone. Ruth continued to ring to try and find out what had happened, but each time Elizabeth hung up on her.

In the end, Elizabeth told her she was not invited to the funeral and gave her no details. Ruth relayed this message to Joe, who by that time was furious at her sister's callousness.

"You don't need an invitation, as she put it. We'll be attending the funeral, if you can find out where and when it is, together."

Ruth rang the local undertakers to find her mum and was at last successful in tracing her body. She visited mum the following day with a small bunch of roses, which she laid in her mum's hands in the coffin. Ruth whispered her thanks and bent over to kiss the only mother she had known.

Alice looked at peace. The funeral director gave Ruth all the information she required and she left with a sad heart.

The day of the funeral arrived and Elizabeth was there with her husband. Her children were also there, and immediately went to Ruth's side to offer comfort to her. Joe and Anne Marie were with Ruth.

It was a short ceremony followed by the cremation, after which they were to go back to the bungalow where Alice had lived, for a snack.

Ruth did not want to go, but was persuaded by her nephew to go regardless of his mother's wishes, telling her that she had more right to be there than his mother, Elizabeth.

Ruth was appalled as she walked into her mum's home; it had been stripped of all her mum's treasured possessions. They were quite worthless, but of sentimental value to Alice. Ruth had expected the home to look just as it normally did until after the funeral.

She was blasted by Elizabeth for not sitting with her dying

mother and Ruth was outraged at this, telling her that she had not known mum was so bad and it had been up to Elizabeth to tell her.

Elizabeth asked everyone apart from Ruth if they wanted anything from the house. Ruth was so distraught that it did not register with her at the time that she was the elder of the two and should have been in charge of her mother's home.

Both Joe and Anne Marie gave Elizabeth a piece of their mind and they all left feeling disgusted at the treatment Ruth had received at the hands of her sister.

A few days later the bungalow was emptied and everything disposed of by Elizabeth to some destination unknown to Ruth.

Ruth arrived at work to be told someone had called and asked for her during the day while she was away. The office staff gave Ruth a small envelope containing a letter and the bill for the funeral expenses that her sister had paid. There was no mention of a will. The letter also stated that the keys had been handed in to the Council and the bungalow was vacant, waiting for the next tenant.

Her revenge had been despicable.

From that day, Ruth no longer had a sister.

CHANGES

Life with Joe brought many changes into Ruth's life. Tracy, Anthony, Joe and Ruth went on holiday together to a caravan at the seaside. All life's luxuries were provided on site. There was evening entertainment for all ages and even the weather smiled on them. They shared laughter at the comedians, ate together, walked on the beach and swam together; a family at last.

What a difference it made to have a partner who enjoyed family life with Ruth. They were all happy.

The following year, Ruth and part of her family flew for the first time in their lives. They boarded the gigantic British Caledonian aircraft through a tunnel, so she did not see the size of the plane until she disembarked. They were beginning a holiday on the beautiful island of Majorca when she stepped onto the tarmac. The size of the huge plane made her gasp.

Ruth enjoyed the flight immensely. Glued to the window for the whole journey, she watched the ground being left far behind as they soared up into the sky. The cloud formations reminded her of snow scenes and fascinated her through the entire journey.

The family party was augmented by Joe's brother and his wife and Anne Marie with her new husband and his son from a previous marriage, as a pal for Anthony. The eight of them booked into a hotel in adjoining rooms.

The weather was glorious, a balmy breeze swaying the pine trees on the promenade as they strolled together in the bright sunshine.

Anthony thoroughly enjoyed himself, along with the other male members of the party, at a fantastic water park. Machines churned the water in huge swimming pools, creating gigantic waves that almost knocked him over.

High flights of steps led to huge slides that none of the females would even attempt to climb. The men did, amid peals of laughter from the girls as they watched them descend with a splash into the pool, sometimes struggling to keep their swimming trunks on, after a great slide back down to the ground.

A visit to a show with dolphins performing their routine tricks brought much applause from the spectators. The zoo alongside had penguins so tame that they could lean over to stroke them, and Ruth found these adorable.

One evening they went to a gigantic barbecue with a pig roast outside. Walls covered with bougainvillea, a beautiful creeping garden vine, hung from every available space, creating a magnificent display.

A great hall was set out with tables in long rows, waiting for the food to be served. Wine flowed freely, served by Spanish waiters dressed in traditional costumes.

The meal was accompanied by a show on a huge stage sparkling with lights and colours. The finale was a magnificent display of dancing waters, shooting high into the air and accompanied by music.

After one evening out they were all strolling along the sea front back to their hotel. The sea looked inviting. Ruth was so hot; the night was still, with hardly a breath of air.

"I'd love to have a dip," she said to Joe.

"Go on then," he replied.

Ruth stepped out of her lightweight dress in a matter of seconds and ran down the beach on impulse. The water was bliss. Joe was behind her and hysterical laughter could be heard from the others, along with shouts of "mother!" from Anne Marie. It was so out of character for Ruth to do such a thing.

Ruth had amazed them all, but it was the best dip in the sea she had ever experienced. She never did live it down; it was referred to for ever after as her 'skinny dip.'

She had never had such a great time before.

The holiday was a great success for all concerned. Ruth arrived home with a fantastic tan and they all looked so well from all the laughter they had shared.

Other holidays abroad followed, in and amongst working at the hospital and returning the garden to its former glory, which was extremely hard work.

The builder had left a huge amount of rubble, which Joe asked for to enable them to make a raised rockery. This meant removing all the soil before burying the rubble beneath it. Slowly the two of them replaced all this, before Ruth started to plant tiny alpines that over the years would spread and cover the rockery.

Gradually a garden began to reappear from a barren wilderness. The greenhouse was repaired, a garden hut erected, the vegetable plot was dug over and the overgrown shrubbery was cut back.

It had all been backbreaking work, but they were rewarded for their efforts as it began to take shape.

Other changes were happening: the family had left home to begin new lives elsewhere. Anthony was working and shared a flat with a workmate. The girls were settling nicely with their new partners, following their weddings.

Ruth was beginning to feel strain in her elbow - not surprising really, with all the work she had been doing of late. She struggled on for a number of weeks until at last she was hardly able to lift anything with that arm.

"I shall have to go to the doctor with this," she told Joe one evening as the pain intensified. She had also noticed a small lump just under her chin, but had asked her charge nurse on the ward for his opinion on that.

"It's just a small swollen gland, I think," he had said, so she was not unduly concerned about that as it did not hurt at all.

On her visit to the doctor, he gave her a cortisone injection in her shoulder. It was not very pleasant at the time, but it certainly cured the tennis elbow. When she mentioned the lump, he showed some concern and told her that he wanted her to go to the infirmary for some tests and X-rays.

This alarmed Ruth a little. Her appointment was through in a matter of days, and it was with some trepidation that she entered the clinic. They took numerous X-rays and poked and prodded her around before finally letting her leave without much information at all.

The following week she was admitted to the hospital for an operation on the lump.

"You have got a perotic tumour," the specialist said. "That is to say, a tumour in your saliva gland. We must take it out straightaway as it may be malignant."

Ruth and Joe were both shocked at this and also extremely worried.

The doctor sat on Ruth's bed the night before the operation was to take place.

"You've been having injections every four hours to thin your blood in case of a thrombosis during surgery," he said. "We have to take great care to make sure that we don't damage any crucial nerves during this operation, which could last two or three hours," he told her. "You will be asked to smile at me when next you wake after the operation, then I'll know whether I've been successful or not. You won't be able to smile if the nerves are damaged too much; it will be as if you've had a stroke."

This information put a great fear into Ruth's mind.

Please God help me through this, she prayed, before spending a sleepless night.

The following morning her hair was shaved away around her ear at the side of her head and Ruth received her pre-med injection. She was given long, white socks to wear, before being wheeled to the theatre for her operation. Her heart was pounding and her head throbbing, mostly due to the lack of sleep the previous night.

The next thing she knew was awaking to find the specialist standing beside her bed. She was violently sick, which continued for a while until the nurse gave her another injection to quell the nausea.

"Smile for me, Ruth, please," the specialist asked, but her face did not seem to belong to her. Her mouth would not work properly; It felt numb all down one side as if she had been to the dentist. Ruth tried to give the smile he had requested, but did not think she had managed it. He smiled back at her, however.

"Well done," he said. "There is a little damage to the nerves, but most of this should disappear in time. We shan't know the full results for six weeks, but I think that I managed to take the whole tumour out. You have eighteen stitches in the side of your face, but these will be taken out later when it has healed. You've been very lucky that we caught it in time."

Ruth thanked him with tears of relief in her eyes. She did feel rather strange, though. When she lay on the side of her face that was operated on, it felt dead. Her neck seemed to have lost its elasticity, making it difficult to hold her head straight. She wanted to look in a mirror to see what it looked like, but was afraid to.

A nurse gave her assurance that she looked all right except for the dressing that stretched from the top of her ear to most of the way down her neck. From the centre of her neck, below her chin, hung a drainage tube into a bag hung from her waist, the contents of which were obnoxious.

"That will be taken out in the next few days, so don't worry," the nurse said.

When she tried to eat she was not in control of her mouth at all. Her lips were numb and her jaw would not perform. The food trickled out each time she tried.

"You'll have to persevere," she was told by the Sister on seeing her difficulty. "It will be easier the more you try."

Joe visited her and was shocked when he saw her. He cuddled her in consolation, which she was glad of.

The tube was removed, which hurt quite a lot; it felt like her head was caving in. Eventually a very nervous nurse removed the stitches, and Ruth was amazed at the neat scar that ran down in a crease from above her ear along her hairline and down her neck.

"You had plastic surgery on it," the Sister said. "The doctor is excellent at it – it's his speciality."

By the time she was discharged, Ruth was so glad that the scar was hardly visible and whispered a prayer of thanks. But she still had to wait six weeks for the results, and that seemed like an eternity.

The weeks passed slowly until the day finally arrived. Joe accompanied her to the hospital and they sat together in the waiting room until her name was called. They entered the treatment room with churning stomachs.

"I'm happy to say that the tumour was not malignant, Ruth," the doctor said. "You'll have to come and see me every year, though, for check-ups, as they can sometimes recur. I hope that won't happen – it's a slim chance only. Take care and goodbye."

Both Ruth and Joe shook his hand and thanked him profusely. They cried with relief on the bus journey home.

It was over.

RECOVERY

To aid Ruth's recovery, Joe booked a holiday in Yugoslavia with very little time to ponder about it. In a matter of weeks, they were off. Ruth was still feeling a little weak and soon felt the cold, due to her blood being so thin. She was getting better by the day, but still the numbness remained in her face.

She was off work for a number of weeks and looked forward to their holiday, her love of flying still with her. Ruth had never been to Yugoslavia but had heard a lot about it from a nurse she worked with who spent every holiday there.

The cleanliness of the place was remarkable and it struck Ruth and Joe how beautiful it was everywhere. The weather was warm during the day but in the evening a chill crept in, as they were facing the sea. The locals called the wind the 'bora.'

The money was difficult to convert as the Dinar was in the thousands to the pound. After booking a few trips out, one to Venice and the other to see the Lipitzana stallions, they had spent in the millions. This caused a lot of laughter between them.

One of the trips was to Lake Bled, a beautiful natural lake surrounded by snow-capped mountains and lush green pine forests. The coach dropped them at the base of a steep path leading to steps that they had to climb up to an inn that resembled a castle.

They arrived eventually in a fairy-tale courtyard, ablaze with colour, the tiled marble floor covered with pots of plants smiling at the sunshine.

Looking over the walls onto the lake, Ruth felt so moved that she filled up with tears. The view was breathtakingly beautiful; the air crystal clear; the water glistening in the sunlight. In the centre of the lake stood a small island with a church that had a red-tipped spire as its centre piece, surrounded by trees. Access to the island was by a small boat moored alongside the lake.

According to the folklore of the island, you were supposed to ring the huge bell in the church tower and make a wish.

Joe and Ruth had paid to make a visit, and along with the others in their party they boarded a boat that glided peacefully across the water, rowed there by the oarsman. Ducks swam alongside quacking, the only sound to be heard apart from the birds and an occasional ripple in the water.

Ruth had never visited such a peaceful place before. It was like a fairy-tale - something one could imagine came from a Disney film - it was so delightful.

She entered the magical church along with her fellow passengers, but try as hard as she might, she could not manage to ring the bell on her first visit. Rather disappointed, she decided to try one more time and at last she heard the peals ring out. Dashing out and grinning from ear to ear, she was just in time to see the camera flash as Joe caught the moment for eternity.

The whole holiday turned out to be a success. She had a gondola ride in Venice and went into the Basilica in St Mark's square to view the mosaics.

They had been on a three-mile train ride deep underground to visit fantastic caves with stalagmites and stalactites. Underground they had walked across a great chasm, on a bridge built by Russian prisoners of war many years before: a masterpiece of engineering.

They had visited the most beautiful place on earth, Lake Bled, watched the magnificent horses perform their act and seen the most spectacular scenery imaginable.

It was a truly memorable holiday that made up for all the past troubles, her only regret being that she was unable to enjoy the lovely crusty bread and all that delicious food served at their hotel.

Ruth would never forget this unbelievable holiday. If anyone had told her a few years before that she would experience such a beautiful time in her life, she would never have believed them.

However, all good things come to an end.

CHALLENGES

On her return to working life, Ruth found that she had been given a new job. The elderly, confused patients she knew had been moved elsewhere and been replaced by psychiatric ones from the local hospital that had been closed down. The ward doors had to be kept permanently locked to stop the patients from wandering outside.

She had been given the job of Activities Organiser and Co-ordinator: a long title for a job she had no idea how to do.

The other staff had nominated her in her absence for the job, as no one else wanted it. The regular staff had been moved, except for the ones who had done a course on mental nursing in their training. The other staff had come from the closed hospital, so some of them knew the patients.

After a week Ruth gave in her notice, as she was despairing about what to do in her new job. The matron would not accept her notice.

"Take a week off, Ruth," she told her. "Get some equipment to work with - you can have access to funds for anything that you need to make your job easier. All I want is for you to keep the patients from getting bored and frustrated, as that's when they get difficult to manage. Some of them will be very co-operative once they've learnt to trust you."

Ruth drew fifty pounds to buy equipment, some of which consisted of tapes and videos. Joe taped all the old films on TV and recorded old-time musicals that she would then be able to play back for the patients. Ruth arranged for a monthly book supplier to call with books suitable for their abilities. A visitor donated a supply of records of old-time songs from the war years, most of which the patients knew.

Ruth went on several training sessions for the nursing of people with mental disabilities. The hospital acquired a coach for the benefit of the patients so Ruth, along with a Staff Nurse, was able to take the most manageable patients out on trips. They went on mini shopping expeditions to the local shop that stocked just about everything imaginable.

One afternoon they took a party of men to the local public house after asking permission from the landlord. The men thoroughly enjoyed it, sticking to no more than a pint each so as not to affect their medication. There was a garden centre nearby, which also had a pet section and aviary along with an aquarium. This was always a favourite trip both for Ruth and her charges. They also visited concerts at the local church by invitation and there were entertainers who were willing to come to the hospital and do a turn.

Ruth was amazed as how much the patients like to dance. Some would sing their heads off whilst the others danced. She had always enjoyed her job at the hospital, but now she found this new one much more interesting.

The matron informed her one day that she wanted the ward rest room to look more like a home than a hospital ward.

"You can go to town and buy furnishings - no expense spared, Ruth, I want it to look like a front room in a house."

Ruth was in her element. Along with the Ward Sister, she purchased new tables and chairs, a fireplace surround and an electric log-effect fire. New curtains were made in the sewing room and pictures hung from the walls. New armchairs had replaced the old high ones that had long been an eyesore around the room. Tablemats were put in place and flowers were on the tables. A relative also provided a budgerigar for the enjoyment of the residents.

The results of the makeover were warmly appreciated by all concerned.

Part III

GRANDCHILDREN

On July 29, 1981 Prince Charles, the heir to the throne, married a beautiful lady named Diana. The event was watched on televisions around the world. The pomp and majesty was unbelievably grand. Their first son was born the following year and was named William.

Miracles were happening in the medical world, with the first heart transplant. The recipient lived for 112 days: a major breakthrough for modern surgery.

Sadness followed with the assassination of Ghandi. Also in the Eighties, the space shuttle Challenger exploded and killed 7 crew, 73 seconds into its ninth launch

The country found it hard to believe when reports came through in 1988 that Pan Am flight 103 had exploded over a small Scottish town named Lockerbie, killing all of the 270 people on board. Libyan terrorists were suspected of placing a bomb on the plane. The Eighties was certainly a decade to be remembered.

Ruth herself heard a startling bit of news in 1983 when Tracy told her that she was to be a grandmother. Ruth was overjoyed and eagerly asked when the baby was due.

"Sometime in the middle of May next year," Tracy replied.

"Good - I have plenty of time to do some knitting before the birth," Ruth told her, already picturing in her mind the beautiful layettes she could make for her first grandchild.

Ruth knitted tiny bootees with matching matinee jackets suitable for either girl or boy. She loved to knit, but had not had any incentive for a long time. Every available minute she would sit and click away with her needles and the quantity of baby-wear soon began to mount.

Time passed, and Tracy was keeping in good health and growing bigger by the week. In the middle of May she produced an adorable girl, who they named Samantha. They were all glad that the babe was perfect.

Tracy turned out to be an excellent mother, dressing the child so prettily. Samantha was a contented baby right from the start and created no problems at all for her mother. Tracy regularly visited Ruth with her child, and Ruth grew to love her baby granddaughter more and more each time she saw her.

Anne Marie, on the other hand, was not the maternal type at all. She was more of a career girl and managed to get an excellent job as Officer Manager for the local branch of Chamber of Commerce. This was a demanding job but Anne Marie sailed through it, enjoying every minute.

In 1988, however, Anne Marie produced Ruth's second grandchild, this time a boy named Danny. Ruth was happy with her daughter's little son and as Anne Marie lived close by she saw him a lot, often babysitting while Anne Marie went out. Anne Marie returned to work, putting her young son in the careful hands of her cousin, who by then had become a registered childminder.

Ruth's life had certainly changed for the better. She loved her job, her home, her garden, and most of all her united family. Joe helped her when she was on shifts, never complaining about the strange hours she kept. As the grandchildren grew older they loved to visit Ruth and they thoroughly enjoyed the huge garden that resembled a park. They had small inflatable paddling pool that came out regularly on their visits in the summer time. Many barbecues were started when the sun shone, but it usually ended up with the rain falling and Joe standing outside alone finishing the cooking.

Ruth and Joe purchased some comfortable garden furniture, which Joe constantly scolded Ruth about as she could not sit still for two minutes without seeing some plant that needed her attention.

Often the children were put in the bath and dressed in their nightclothes before being taken home by mum and dad, the children usually complaining bitterly. They had some wonderful times together in Ruth's own little haven.

This was not to last, however.

Samantha was still under school age when Tracy decided to buy a larger house. She had found herself a job to help pay for the extra expense that would be involved, working as cash-out assistant in the town's supermarket.

Unbeknown to her husband, she began to have an affair with the bakery manager of the store. The new house was ready for completion when Tracy decided to leave the marital home. The purchase of the new house had be cancelled, costing Tracy's husband quite a lot of money due to the breach of contract.

Tracy kept Samantha living with her while her husband went back to live with his parents. She still visited Ruth, bringing Samantha with her and leaving her there. Her daddy would pick her up to take her home to his parents' house for the day, then return her to Ruth's for her mother to pick up later. The change did not seem to affect the child at all.

On one of her visits to her Nana's, Samantha was playing in the garden as usual. She was dressed up in Joe's cap and coat, a favourite pastime of hers, when a plane flew overhead.

"My mummy's on that plane, granddad," she told Joe. He agreed with her, thinking it was only childish fantasy.

Later that evening when her father collected Samantha, he was unable to return her to her mother's house as he usually did because she was not at home. He returned a number of times to the house, with the same result. In the end he phoned Ruth.

"Have you any idea where Tracy is?" he asked anxiously, for it was getting late.

Joe remembered Samantha's words about the plane.

"Ask Samantha about her mummy," Joe told him. Samantha told her daddy that her mummy had gone to Spain for her holiday.

It was no childish fantasy, as it turned out. Tracy had indeed gone to Spain as Samantha had said, without a word to anyone except the child. Ruth felt a mixture of emotions: shock, anger and disgust; even shame that a daughter of hers could treat a small child in that way.

For Tracy to fly to another country without warning and without any arrangements being made for the welfare of her daughter shook Ruth to the core. She could not understand the motives behind Tracy's actions.

Alice had loved Ruth and Elizabeth as a true mother, without any selfish motives in mind. How could Tracy - her own flesh and blood - deny Samantha the love and devotion she so rightly deserved? How could she just pass her responsibilities on to someone else without a thought of how it would inconvenience them?

From that day, Ruth's son-in-law applied for custody of his daughter and Samantha went to live with him permanently at his parents' house.

Samantha loved her chubby, cuddly grandmother and granddad. She settled down well with them, but they lived quite a distance away in the countryside. It was a very nice area, surrounded by farms and Samantha had a different way of life to the one she had had with her mum. Her grandmother had to change her life to accommodate the child. Up to then she had had a job, but it was impossible for her to continue working and care for Samantha so she gave her notice to her employers. The house also had to be rearranged for the child to provide her with a bedroom of her own.

None of this bothered either Samantha or her cuddly grandma, who took it all in her stride and enjoyed the child's presence around the house. Samantha certainly brightened up a dull day with her laughter.

Ruth and Joe still had contact with their granddaughter on the weekends, but not as often as they had had before. Ruth was still working but her shifts had changed to full days instead of the normal rota she had been used to. Joe had finished with the Territorial Army but still worked for the Army as a civilian employee. They continued to attend the regimental functions as usual. He was still very much involved with army life, but did not go away on exercises any more. They visited the local public house on weekend evenings, making many new friends.

An old friend of Joe's turned up on one such evening.

"My brother is going to open a bar in Spain," his friend told him.

Joe told them about their visit to Majorca and how Ruth had fallen in love with the Spanish way of life. They had talked about moving there when they retired.

"Let me know how your brother gets on – I'm quite curious," Joe said.

Joe's friend brought his wife the next time and introduced her to Ruth. She seemed pleasant enough and they had quite a few laughs. They met each other most weekends after that, and spent some happy times together.

A number of months later the brother returned from Spain with very good reports on his success. After a few pints, they discussed the idea of going before they retired, but to Greece instead of Spain.

"Shall we go on holiday to Greece and have a look round next summer?" Joe's friend asked.

They agreed, and a booking was made for a fortnight's holiday on one of the Greek islands for the following summer.

NEW HORIZONS

The time finally arrived for the holiday in Greece. They had talked many times during the last few months of what they would like to do if they did go to live there. They would have to sell both houses before they could even contemplate going. That would be a very hard thing for Ruth to do, as would giving up the job she loved so much.

Ruth was not quite as enthusiastic as the rest of them at the idea of leaving everything behind to start a new life elsewhere, but went along with it as Joe seemed really set on it. She decided it would have to prove really special for her to agree to go and live there permanently and leave all her family. It would need very careful consideration on her part.

The others in the group seemed so elated at the idea as they waited to board the plane that Ruth didn't voice her feelings about it at all. They faced an eight-hour delay before they could fly, due to some technical problem with the plane. This did not improve Ruth's anxiety at all.

They faced another eight-hour wait for the tiny island hopper plane to take them to the island when they finally did arrive in Athens. Ruth was beginning to feel that this was not meant to be as she walked around the city, feeling very tired. It was extremely noisy, with lane upon lane of fast-moving traffic. The smell of exhaust fumes invaded her nose and eyes. She was not impressed at all.

The views changed dramatically as they approached the island they were to visit. The sea was glistening in the sunlight, a beautiful aquamarine colour. Quaint buildings lined the harbour walls; a ferry lay moored at anchor against the quay. People were strolling around the waterside cafes and shops. Ruth could see churches perched high on mountaintops, surrounded by pine trees. Orange and lemon groves mingled among the olive trees wherever she looked from her seat on the plane, and small blue and white traditional Greek cottages were dotted around between the large holiday complexes.

She began to change her mind - perhaps it could be quite an adventure here after all.

The plane landed and they could feel the heat as they descended the steps to the ground. The sun was shining brilliantly as they made their way through Customs. After collecting their luggage from the carousel in the airport, they booked into their hotel.

Although they were all very tired, they could not resist going out into the warm sunshine for a walk. The sea looked crystal clear and a warm breeze drifted over them as they made their way to a man-made lido on top of the rocky beach. Sun beds were arranged for their use, and a cafe was situated to the right of the area. They each bought a drink and made themselves comfortable on the inviting sun beds.

During the week they arranged to meet an agent who would show them round various properties in the area. Some were for sale, others were to rent. They had a very comprehensive tour all round the small island, and the more Ruth saw the more she liked it.

Some of the tourist parts were a little over commercialised, but others were secluded. There were many tourists spending their holidays on the beautiful island, many riding around on small scooters. The driving of the Greek motorists, however, left a lot to be desired. They did not seem to have any system for driving on the main roads; anything was allowed. Quite dangerous risks were taken with the traffic, it seemed to Ruth, who was used to English roads.

The holiday was very nice when they had time to enjoy it. The Greek people were very friendly; most of them very obliging. Ruth enjoyed the Greek food tremendously - even though it looked as if it were swimming in oil, it didn't seem to taste like it. Fruit grew in abundance on the island and flowers were displayed all over the town and countryside.

Goats, dogs, chickens and cats roamed around wild and there were plenty of donkeys, but most of them were being used to pull heavy loads of sticks or sacks. All the dogs and goats were tethered on long chains with very little shade at all, which Ruth was a little sad about as she loved dogs herself and thought they should be free. She learned later that the reason for this was that the island had snakes, although luckily she did not see any.

They were introduced to an English couple who lived on the island. The man had built his own house and he made them very welcome. He had his own small olive grove beside the house that he said made him a little cash in the winter time when he harvested the olives. The main crop of the island was the currant harvest, which was usually exported to countries like England. Work could be found helping during the olive picking or the currant season, he informed them.

The goats were reared to be eaten, along with the chickens, and most of the farmers also had rabbits. The town was, however, stocking more and more English commodities as quite a number of English lived on the island permanently. Most of them had their own businesses, some of them open all year round.

Ruth thought that maybe this would be all right, but she did not really want to live the English way; she would rather get away from that. The Greek people seemed to have a relaxed lifestyle that appealed more to her.

She would love to wander around her own garden, growing her aubergines, courgettes and tomatoes in the Greek sun. Perhaps she could have a few chickens for some eggs, but she was not so sure about the goat. It would be rather nice to be able to wander in the orange grove and pick a fresh grown orange from their own trees.

She was sold on the idea of living in Greece by the time it was time for them to leave. Ruth felt much happier about it all, and much more willing to give it a try. She had fallen for the island and its charm. Its name was the 'island of flowers,' and it certainly lived up to its name.

She would go home and put her house on the market. The plan was for whoever sold their house first to move in with the other couple until they could all leave together. First they would buy a caravan to take their household goods to Greece, and the other couple would supply the car to tow it. The idea was to go by road and make it a journey of adventure journey through other countries. When they returned to England, both couples put their respective homes on the market. Ruth and Joe purchased a caravan with an awning, making it big enough to sleep all four. Two would sleep in the caravan and the other two in the awning attached to the caravan.

The next thing to do was to visit the Greek Consulate in England and look into the ins and outs of their proposed adventure. Each time they went it cost money for special stamps of approval on their passports and details of their intentions. They had a triple list of everything they were taking - one for the Consulate, one for themselves and the other for Customs.

The houses did not sell as fast as they would have liked, as the housing market was in a slump. The mortgage rate was very high and there was talk about government changes. Ruth found that her large garden, as beautiful as it was, became something of a bugbear since some prospective buyers thought it too big. Others thought the bungalow too small. Their friends were having trouble as well, as their house was on a main road with buses constantly passing and the road was used as a racetrack half the time.

It was almost a year before a sale was finally agreed on Ruth's bungalow. They packed the caravan with all their goods and moved into the friends' house. Joe slept in the caravan whilst Ruth slept on the floor in a small box room. The women shopped together, halving the cost, and sharing the household tasks.

Ruth decided that maybe the idea of living together was not a good one. She began to dislike the way her female friend tried to order her around, yet she could do nothing about it as she was a guest in her house. The only place to call her own was the caravan, and that was packed up with all her worldly goods, except for the packing cases that were in her friends' front room waiting for the day they could be sent off in transit.

It had passed the point of no return, but Joe did not realise that the situation was not as it should be. Ruth did not want to worry him, but by now she felt sure that she was making the worst mistake of her life.

FAREWELL

Ruth and Joe could hardly wait for their departure from troubled England in the Nineties.

Problems in Kuwait following the invasion by Iraq were met by the UN, who started a campaign to liberate Kuwait, resulting in the killing of 200,000 Iraqi people. The Soviet Union ceased to be. The Queen suffered a disastrous fire at Windsor Castle. In America, President Clinton was elected. Jackie, the former wife of John F Kennedy, died and was buried beside him. Charles and Diana were to divorce.

Both Ruth and Joe were looking forward to the peace of their chosen island. The day of departure arrived, the final farewells having been made the previous night. A party had been arranged for relatives and friends on both sides. The AA had been consulted and a detailed route had been planned. Every consideration had been given to details such as low bridges, hills and so on to ensure that the route was suitable for towing a caravan. The two men had spent hours perusing this.

Their journey was planned to take them from Yorkshire down to Dover for the ferry to take them over to France. The next country would be Germany, then down the Rhine valley, through the Alps into Italy and then down to Brindisi for the ferry crossing to Patras. The whole journey had been planned as a great sightseeing expedition. A great adventure, probably never to be ventured again.

All the invited guests turned up for the final farewell except Tracy. Ruth was very perturbed by this, remembering Tracy's words when she had first told her their intentions.

"You mean you're selling my inheritance," she had said. This was not what Ruth had expected from her.

Anne Marie had been both happy and sad for her mother when she had been told, but wished her well regardless. Anthony had cried on the final night, much to Ruth's dismay, as she had not seen him cry since he was a young child.

The biggest wrench for Ruth was leaving her grandchildren. The final farewell had been planned so that they could set off in the morning with no tearful goodbyes.

After a sleepless night and an early breakfast at 8.30, the four of them, complete with car and caravan, left at 9.30 for their journey to the ferry. They hit a traffic jam due to an accident on a roundabout involving a tanker and large van that had collided with each other. The delay was not too long, however, and soon they were away again, seeing their first thatched cottage around 11 o'clock.

They stopped for lunch before entering the Dartford tunnel, then carried on to Dover for a night in a hotel, spending their last night in England before catching the morning ferry.

As they watched the white cliffs of Dover slip away into the distance, Ruth did not really know how she felt. She had spent a very sad journey up to then due to seeing Anne Marie and her grandson just as they were leaving that morning.

The crossing was uneventful and they disembarked around lunchtime in Calais. The weather was very warm and sunny. The roads were very good, better than English ones, but they soon became very monotonous with little to see apart from acres upon acres of sunflowers.

The back of the car was exceedingly hot in the midday sun. By the time they reached the Chalon-Sur-Mur campsite, each of them was eager to have a shower. There was unfortunately nowhere open to obtain any food; all that was available was a vending machine for cold drinks.

All the other occupants of the caravans and trailers seemed to have settled down for the night, as there was no one to be seen. There was nothing else to do but settle down in the caravan for the night, but it was quite cramped. It was not much fun being hungry, either.

They were on the road again the following morning at 9.30, driving further into France on the same monotonous roads towards

Champignoile Dura Dist, to a campsite with a swimming pool this time. After their evening meal, once again there was nothing to do so they had another early night, but this time with the awning erected.

The following day they were leaving France and heading for Geneva. After crossing the French border they travelled into Switzerland to go through the Mont Blanc tunnel. The scenery improved greatly, with snow capped mountains stretching into Chamoniz. They parked the vehicles and had a wander around the beautiful place, seeing the ski lifts and ski runs. The soft drinks they purchased were exceedingly expensive. It was a very beautiful area, with small chalets peeping out of the mountainsides; very picturesque. After a short rest there, they travelled on into Italy, arriving at 6.20 in the evening, very tired. That day they had covered a lot of miles.

They found a small hotel and booked in for two days' rest, but again they were too late for the evening meal. The hotelier was very obliging, however, and sent out for pizzas for them. They ate and drank and chatted before going to bed early again.

Two whole days' rest made a welcome relief from sitting melting in the back seat of the car. Ruth was happy to feel the fresh, clean air for a change, as they traced a waterfall back up a slope, the flow of which had originated back in the mountain they had just come through the previous day.

The area was steep but very pleasant, with a gentle breeze blowing as they strolled around the pretty village. Small chalets, their balconies covered with flowers, greeted them everywhere they looked. Walking around in the sun, they were all tanning nicely without really trying. The rest did them all good as it was getting a little tedious travelling all the time.

The original route that had taken so long to plan had been abandoned, much to Ruth's disappointment. She had not travelled in any of the countries they had intended to visit; the driver changed his mind just when he felt like it and he did not care what others thought. As they were not able to drive themselves, Joe and Ruth had to go along with his wishes.

Another day dawned with bright sunshine streaming through the hotel windows. Away they went, after having a continental breakfast of jam and bread, this time heading for Alessandria on the way to San Marco. They found the only available hotel in which to stay the night. It looked very expensive but they had no choice as it was getting very late. The following morning they paid the bill of £100, after searching for a bank as they did not have enough Italian Lira.

The party then headed for Ancona and the ferry that would take them to Patras. They saw the first glimpse of the sea at 1.45 that day as they boarded the 'Meditteranean Sky,' a huge passenger liner. They were to spend two days aboard, Ruth praying that it would be smooth as she was not a very good sailor. Her prayers were not answered this time for they had not been on board for long before the crew began to empty the two large swimming pools on deck.

The wind began to blow and the boat began to rock; she was not looking forward to this journey. In the evening, after an excellent meal which she managed to keep down, they watched a display of Greek dancing in the lower deck lounge. The rocking could not be felt down there so much. Each couple had ordered a cabin so they could have a shower, and they could get into a bed even though it was only a bunk.

The next morning it was very hot on board and Ruth and Joe went up on deck, which was very pleasant. The breeze was lovely and the sea was calmer. After another night on board, they finally arrived in Patras at 9.00am. The weather was again lovely. They made their way through Customs, which was confusing to say the least.

Now they were on Greek soil and heading by road to Killini for the ferry to take them through to the island on which they had chosen to spend the rest of their lives.

The small island ferry began to cruise across the clear turquoise waters, so clear that they could almost see the bottom of the ocean. It was a delightful journey. Dolphins were swimming alongside the boat, enjoying themselves in the bubbles from the rudder. Each one seemed to have a smile on its face as it played. Ruth was enthralled at their antics. Soon the picturesque houses, churches and shops came into view as they approached the island.

This truly was the nicest part of the whole journey.

LIFE ANEW

They had arranged to visit the English couple they had met on their previous visit, leaving the caravan whilst they attended to the accommodation they would all need. A small Greek cottage, vacant the previous year, was available across the road from the English couple. They had approached the owner had been approached about renting it the year before and a sort of agreement had been made that if it was still available when they returned, they could have it. They had not expected to be so long selling their homes.

They were disappointed, however, as the English couple were not at home and the cottage looked as if it were occupied. Not knowing quite what to do, the driver took them all, complete with caravan, to a place he and his wife had stayed on numerous occasions as tourists. The Greek people, who he knew, agreed that he could park the caravan on their land if they rented two rent rooms from them, which they did.

Their next project was to set up a Greek bank account, as they had left all their money banked in England. Then they would have to try and find alternative accommodation before they could accept the huge packing cases that had been sent to Greece just prior to their leaving England. All they owned was in these cases, and they had been given a time limit on how long they had before finding an address.

The four of them re-traced their way to the English couples' house and this time found them home. They were greeted warmly

In the evening the four of them went to the nearest resort to visit acquaintances of the driver and his wife, who they had met while on holidays in Greece previously and to have a good meal. After they had eaten, the couple brought out a pack of cards. Joe joined them in the card games while Ruth had to sit back because she did not know how to play. Her father had not allowed a pack of cards in the house when she was younger. He had always said they were the work of the devil and they were taboo in his home.

This situation carried on for hours. While the others played, Ruth grew more and more depressed. She started thinking of what she had left behind; she had certainly not left her old life just to sit in a beach bar playing cards all night.

Her priority was to find a home on the island. Joe and the others ganged up on her for looking so miserable and she got up and walked away, the tears very near.

As she wandered among the happy holidaymakers, she began to think that living here with the other three was not what she wanted after all. She returned to the group, who by that time had drunk quite a few pints. Joe walked away from her with the others and left her sitting alone. She began to walk up the street, but there was no sign of them so she made her way back to the rented room. Joe returned a while later and berated her for her silliness.

During the next few days they toured round with the help of the Greek friends of the driver and his wife, looking for accommodation. Eventually some was found for the other couple, but not Joe and Ruth. They moved into their new abode taking the car with them leaving Joe and Ruth stranded with the caravan. Once they were settled they seemed to be reluctant to assist Ruth and Joe to find their future home. Ruth saw very little of them, so together with Joe, she hired a bike and went to visit the English couple.

They proved most helpful, introducing them both to a Greek man named Dionysus who was building some rooms to rent nearby. He had two apartments finished, one for himself to live in and the other vacant. They arranged the terms for renting and were made very welcome.

The caravan was still at the other place but now they had no means of moving it without the assistance of the couple with whom they had travelled.

An offer was made to them from the Greek owners of the rented rooms to purchase the caravan. They wanted to use it as an office to start a business renting bikes to tourists. The price was much lower that the caravan was worth, but in the circumstances they agreed to sell. This would eliminate the importation charges, which was one less thing to worry about.

Dionysus arranged to go to the town with them to draw up a contract for the renting of his property. He also agreed to help them buy some furnishings they would need. The apartment had already got three rooms furnished with beds and built in wardrobes. The most important items they would need were a cooker and a fridge. Dionysus had lived in Australia for a number of years, so he spoke with a comical accent that was both English and Australian

He was a pleasant man and helped them to translate into Greek what they needed to say. The furniture was to be delivered later that afternoon. Ruth and Joe visited the other couple to tell them what was arranged and they stayed for a while with the promise that they would give Ruth a lift, as they also were going to the stores for some things.

Joe went back to the apartment on the bike. On Ruth's return, Dionysus came running out to the car to tell her Joe had been in an accident.

"There is blood all over," he said, frightening Ruth who immediately ran into the apartment. Joe was in a bit of a state and there was blood all over him, but it was mingled with some red coloured spray someone had put on him, making it look twice as bad.

He had braked and shot over the handlebars onto the road. Some Greek people living nearby had rushed out to his assistance. The Greeks always used this red antiseptic spray in emergencies, they later discovered. Luckily Ruth had a supply of medical goods with her, so between them they managed to put dressings on his injuries. It took quite a while before he was properly healed, but at least he was still with her. It made Ruth think about their situation, though. What if he had been killed? What would she have done?

Dionysus took them up the road to the local café in the evening and introduced them to the owner's wife. One by one the local farmers came to call, each one pulling up a chair until they formed a half-circle around Ruth and Joe. No one could speak English. They stared at this typical English woman, dressed in her English clothes complete with make-up. Ruth was very embarrassed and did not know what to do except smile. She was rather glad when Joe eventually said suggested that they went home, feeling that she had been a curiosity for long enough.

Their goods were stranded in Piraeus due to a ferry strike and had been put into storage. When eventually the goods did arrive, it cost more money than they thought to get them back. The Customs man arrived at the apartment with his board and the packing cases and the list of contents with which he had been supplied from England

He held out his hand for the charges of 18 per cent tax on everything they had shipped, plus storage. This was not what they had been told in England. No tax should have been due according to the Greek Consul at home. They could not have the cases until they paid up, however, so a large amount of money changed hands that day, much to their regret.

They had only been in Greece for a couple of weeks when Anne Marie told her during a phone call home that she was coming to visit on a fortnight's holiday, bringing her mother-in-law. Ruth had the beds but no sheets and decided to go to the town to purchase some with Joe on the bike. Ruth was not too happy about riding on the bike but Joe promised he would be careful, as now he knew what not to do.

After scouring the shops to no avail, unable to translate what they needed into Greek, they decided to go home. On their way they saw a market with what looked like rolls of material.

"Joe, pull over there and let's see if it's suitable for sheets," Ruth asked in desperation.

The trouble was she did not know how much material to buy. She tried to work it out by holding her arm away from her nose, thinking that it would be roughly one yard. She counted up how many she would need and purchased the cotton material.

That evening she got out her sewing machine and began to sew the sheets while Joe was out at the local cafe having a drink.

"I've just seen you on the TV in the cafe, Ruth," he said on his return. She laughed, thinking he was having a joke with her.

"It's true! The locals said, 'look at Mrs Ruth on TV,' and when I looked at it, you were. When we were at the market this afternoon they must have had a camera somewhere filming it. You were there for all to see, waving your arms backwards and forwards and counting."

"Oh! Goodness me, I'm glad I wasn't in the cafe tonight, I would have been so embarrassed."

"I wouldn't worry about that, Ruth, it's endeared you to the locals."

THE ISLAND

Life was certainly different on the island. Each morning Ruth and Joe were rudely awakened by the sound of the cocks crowing in the early hours. These would then wake the donkeys, that began to bray. Each morning the sun was blazing through the bedroom window, the heat of it not quite at its highest in the early morning.

The apartment had a balcony running across the front, so Ruth and Joe would take their morning cup of tea and sit and watch the local farmers going about their chores.

Across the road lived an elderly couple. Each morning the old lady would bring out a buffet and start to milk the goat in the front garden. Gradually she began to wave to them. They could speak no Greek and she could not speak English, so they didn't have any conversation with her at all. Her husband would raise his hand and shout 'Yasu' as he went along the road with his donkey loaded with sticks. It wasn't long before all the villagers would do the same as they realised that the English couple had come to stay.

Dionysus, who asked to be called Niso, did the best he could, telling them all about the village. Many a happy hour was spent in his company.

Anne Marie came to stay with her husband and Danny as promised, bringing the mother-in-law. They were very pleased to see that Ruth and Joe were nicely settled. Anne Marie said that she had been exceedingly worried about her mum, so she just had to come and visit to make sure everything was all right.

The weather was good for their visit, with hot sun during the day and pleasant evenings. The island was a popular place for tourists to visit, with low prices and many bars spread along the shoreline, ideal for families with young children. The beaches were safe due to the low water level stretching out quite along way, with little tide change to speak of.

Most of the tourists visited a particular area which had bars run by English ex-pats playing all manner of loud music. To Ruth and Joe it was very much like visiting Blackpool and they hated it. They preferred the beach on the other side of the island, used by the Greeks.

There were such lovely deserted beaches, as yet undiscovered by the tourists, on which one could spend all day in peace and quiet. The town was one long stretch of shops, all selling the usual tourist paraphernalia, the most popular of which were the beautiful lace tablecloths and the statuettes of beautiful ladies in Grecian robes. Tea cloths showing a map of the island were everywhere to be seen, along with recipe books of Greek food.

Along the seafront the ferry came in from Piraeus each day and the local fishing boats brought in the latest catch for the locals. On the main stretch of road was the church of St Dionysus, the patron saint of the island. On one particular day in the year on the feast of St Dionysus, his mummified body, which was around 600 years old, was paraded through the streets with all the islanders following in a great procession. The tradition was that they had to kiss his shoes each year. It was a very special day for everyone on the island.

The local inhabitants used all manner of transport to reach the town. Many a time a motorbike would pass by with a local sitting side-saddle, holding a gas bottle on their knees, behind the driver. Crates were wired onto the backs of bikes to carry goods purchased in the town. One large area in a square was covered with tables and chairs so the tourists were able to enjoy their meals in the open air.

The town closed down for the afternoon, reopening in the evening when the sun was not quite so hot. It would then come alive with Greek families taking their children out when it was cooler. It did seem rather strange to Ruth to see so many children out at night, yet the streets were all brightly lit and all the shops were open. Great family gatherings seemed to take place every evening. The island seemed to have something magical about it.

One thing that took Ruth and Joe a long time to get used to was the fact that the local male population always seemed to be carrying an assortment of firearms. They regularly awoke to the sound of gunshots. It took a while to discover that the hunting season was in full swing and any bird was fair game to be shot and taken home for a meal.

On their visits to the town they would call in at the local English bar that stayed open all winter, usually to get warm again after the bike ride. They discovered that it was run like an English bar, with the usual darts and dominoes league. The friends with whom they had travelled were part of the teams, but it was not what Ruth and Joe wanted; they had come to Greece to live with the Greeks and that is what they did.

They were always welcome at the local cafe, which was also the local bread supplier. It sold groceries such as flour, sugar and tea, and all manners of drinks and ices. It was also the local butcher's. When there was a beast to be killed, it was done on the spot before being put into a large freezer for distribution later. In the evenings it was a bar and meeting place for the local farmers after their hard day's work.

None of them drank to excess, in fact they drunk very little. One person bought a bottle of beer and then it was passed round between everyone until someone else bought the next, and so on.

The local cafe also took in all the mail from the town and had a telephone line for anyone to use. There was nothing grand about the place, most of the customers sitting on a hard bench covered in rags. One or two chairs were available around a large table covered with a waterproof covering. Ruth and Joe always managed to get a chair each, as the owner always told whoever was sitting on them to move, which they always politely did.

The owners had also lived in Australia at some time but had forgotten how to speak English since their return to the island. Their son could speak English, however. He was employed delivering drinks to the tourist areas, but on occasions he would be in the cafe translating for Ruth and Joe. They gratefully appreciated this as it gave them a chance to converse with the locals, albeit a little slowly, but it was better than nothing.

Christmas was soon approaching and Ruth was beginning to feel a little homesick.

Sula, the cafe owner's wife, was beginning to learn a little English again and asked Ruth about her family. Between sign language and drawing, they were able to have little conversations together.

On one of Ruth's visits, Sula invited both Ruth and Joe to share Christmas dinner with her and her family, which they gratefully accepted. The last week before Christmas, Ruth asked Joe to take her to the town. They bought a Christmas tree, lights and a few decorations which they put in front of their patio window for all to see as they passed. It made it seem a little more like Christmas, even though the weather was still warm and sunny during the day. After four o'clock, however, the sun dropped behind the mountains and a distinct chill set in.

The sky at night was a picture. Ruth had never seen so many stars shining so brightly night after night. Occasionally she would see a shooting star. The moon was always very bright and the need for street lighting was minimal.

Bats would dive around any lights there were, and in the evenings the little lizards came out to play. It was quite pleasant to watch them against the buildings, eating the small gnats that congregated around the lights in the evenings. Crickets could be heard among the grape vines and pine trees that covered the island, singing their songs night after night. It took some getting used to, but eventually they barely noticed them.

The local boys of teenage years spent a lot of their time riding around on bikes in the evenings, so it was not very peaceful really. Girls were very seldom seen, as most of them spent their time crocheting beautiful lace for their dowry. All the marriages were arranged between the parents of both families.

On Christmas day, Ruth and Joe dressed in smart clothes for their visit for lunch. They received a very nice welcome. They were each handed a drink and asked to sit down. In the room, a large table was set with a pretty cover. Wine glasses were in place and the owner's home-brewed wine took pride of place in the centre. Everyone had a sip and wished each other merry Christmas.

Sula proceeded to bring out dishes, followed by a large soup tureen brimming over with a yellow soup. She served each of them, filling their bowls to the top. Ruth noticed as she did so that there was rice in the soup. This was the traditional Greek meal for Christmas, called Avra Lemoni, made from meat stock with boiled rice and quite a lot of eggs beaten into it, giving it the yellow colouring. It was very filling, accompanied by chunks of crusty bread torn off a large roll.

The next course was the meat, which was placed in the centre of the table and everyone just tucked in. The meat looked terrible - all grey, boiled alone in water without any flavouring at all - but it tasted much better than it looked.

After the meal all the dishes were cleared away and after more wine the door was opened for the locals to call. The usual card games followed just like any other evening, so Joe and his wife took their leave, thanking their host very much.

It had been a very kind gesture to invite them, knowing how Ruth must have been feeling on her first Christmas away from her loved ones, and she was very grateful.

It was certainly different; a Christmas to be remembered.

SPRINGTIME

Slowly the mist crept down the mountainside on a cold mid-February afternoon. The rain was splashing heavily on the surface of the ground, lying in huge pools mirroring the sky with its heavily laden clouds.

It had been eight weeks since the last rain and the earth was baked dry by the harsh, drying winter winds and the previous summer's sun. The rumble of distant thunder could be heard and great flashes of lightening, illuminating everything around, were frightening to watch. The mist rolled down the mountainside and a final outburst of heavy rain sent every man and beast running for shelter.

Following the rain, the sun came out and the trees, thankful for their drink, suddenly came to life once more. The delicate pink blossom of the almond trees, etched against the dull grey sky, brought a promise of spring about to be reborn. The variegated greens of the citrus trees, their branches heavily laden with fruit, were a sharp contrast against the bare, twiggy apple trees. The acres of grapevines with their brown stalks spread out like upturned umbrellas to the sky.

It was hard to believe that in a few months' time, the farmers would be filling their baskets to the brim with grapes from them. Some grapes were for dessert, others were dried for sale at supermarkets around the world as currants. Most of the crop nearest the property was made into house wine for personal use from one year to the next.

A great deal of preparation was put into the grape growing. They had to be constantly sprayed whilst the dew was still on them to stop the attack from midges that would destroy the fruit. The farmer erected wooden fences in rows to form tunnels, over which he placed huge sheets to protect the grapes in case it began to rain. The farmer would spend hours, first picking and then laying the grapes

R D Payne

onto sheets spread on the ground to dry in the strong summer sun. He spent days turning the grapes over and raking them, removing the stalks as they dried, most of the time surrounded by wasps eager to sample the rich grape juice before anyone else got the chance.

When they were all dry he collected them into large sacks and sent them to the factory to be cleaned and packed before being exported and ending up on a supermarket shelf labelled 'currants, produce of Greece.'

Ruth began to love this beautiful island in the Ionian Sea, a one-and-a-half hour ferry ride from the Greek mainland. Its breathtaking beauty had captured her heart and awakened a yearning to know it better. The majestic pines and the heavenly scent of orange blossom mingled with jasmine among the brilliantly coloured flowers in the summer time. Quaint white cottages with red roofs were tucked into hollows on the mountainsides, surrounded by the colours of Greece. Geraniums were ablaze with cerise, pinks and reds blooming all summer long.

The contrasting trees: olives, magnificent eucalyptus and tall towering poplars, created a beauty of nature one could never tire of. Long stretches of beach were covered with sand as soft as flour and almost as white. Gentle waves lapped to and fro in shallow water. Natural bays unspoilt by human hand, with crystal clear water, were ever changing from the deepest blue to aquamarine in the sunlight.

High on the hilltops stood the churches, land marks for all to see, silently watching over the quiet countryside until the papas summoned his worshippers to service.

White-painted bell towers glistened in the bright sunlight of summer; symbols of the ancient gods revered by the Greek people and whose spirits still lived on in Greece.

Wild flowers covered the olive groves in the spring with a heavy perfume unlike any other flower. Freesias grew wild along with garlic, grape hyacinths, spinach and rosemary shrubs. Wild sage was a cure for colds made into an infusion and drunk. Pomegranate trees displayed bright red flowers before setting the huge fruits. Everything grew much larger than Ruth had ever seen it before, especially the weeds.

Ruth and Joe explored the whole island, up the hills and down to the quiet coves on their motorbike. They went high into the mountains, travelling among the pines, whose heavenly scent lingered in the air. From the highest points they could see the sea all around the island. Spectacular views stretching for miles greeted them from every vantage point. They strolled along deserted beaches, picking up driftwood for Joe to work with when he had time during the rain sessions. Occasionally they would take off their shoes and stroll through the water's edge. The water was cool, but not cold, and very refreshing.

Ruth and Joe found the peace and tranquillity of the island so relaxing compared to the hectic pace of life they had left behind in England. Each day they enjoyed their life there more and more. As the locals began to recognise them, the invitations to people's homes began to come more frequently.

When a wedding was arranged in the village they were invited to the girl's party, which was similar to the hen nights in England except for the fact that all the village was invited, both males and females. On arrival at the girl's home a drink was put into their hands and they were shown around a room that had been emptied of furniture.

Covering the walls was an array of needlework worked by the girl during her younger years. The exquisite crocheted goods made Ruth gasp and feel a little ashamed that she could not make any herself. Usually it was not very often that the girls were seen outside their own homes. Ruth realised why when she saw the amount of needlework the girl had made. There was table linen, bed linen, handkerchiefs, lace-edged towels, dressing table sets and all manner of household requirements, enough to last a lifetime.

On one wall the dress the girl would be wearing at her wedding was on show for all to see. Her other garments were also displayed so that everyone in the village would know what all her items of underwear looked like.

The party was in full swing with a small group of musicians, one playing a keyboard, another with drums and one with cymbals. The music was not unfamiliar; an arrangement of 'Roll out the Barrel,' Greek style, was heard a few times. This greatly amused both Ruth and Joe so they decided to do a little dance to it and their neighbours applauded them loudly. A great evening was had by all with plenty of wine, beer and food for everyone.

The following evening there was a party for the lucky lad. The same thing applied; all the village was invited. It was all drink and fun with plenty of dancing for the exact same group as the night before, with the exact same music also. The men danced the more traditional Greek dances, waving a white handkerchief around as they jumped up and down. Circles were formed, growing bigger and bigger as the dance progressed. Usually everyone went home again a little the worse for drink on such occasions.

The wedding day followed, with once again the whole village in attendance. Some went to the church in cars, throwing almonds wrapped in small pretty sachets to anyone around. Others travelled on tractors or on donkeys and some on motorbikes, in fact on anything that would move. The noise was deafening as each conveyance sounded its horn. Joe and Ruth did go into the church, but watched the service from the organ loft above There were so many lighted candles, carried a little carelessly, that Ruth was a little afraid that some of the beautiful lace outfits would be set ablaze.

The actual wedding service seemed to go on for ages, with the papa waving rings with ribbon streamers over the heads of the bride and groom and changing them over and over again. When it was finally over the guns could be heard firing once again.

The usual party for the village followed at the groom's home, where he and his bride were expected to live from then on. The nuptial bed was on display with the brides wedding nightwear laid across it, the bed covers strewn with rose petals.

Christenings were also a village occasion, with everyone present but without the entertainment the night before. The fun started after the service. Ruth wondered if the babies had nervous dispositions, as so many guns were fired after any celebration.

The best event they went to was at Easter. On Good Friday everyone was sad, but at midnight on the Saturday the whole place erupted with noise of every description. Guns went off, church bells rang out and vehicles sounded their horns. The entire village was at the church when midnight approached, all clutching candles.

The papa came out with his black robes on, carrying a lighted candle, from which he proceeded to light every other person's candle. They each took their candle home. If it remained lit, it was a good omen according to village custom.

On the Monday, a great feast was prepared for all to join. The now familiar entertainment group was in attendance as Ruth and Joe joined their fellow Greeks at the party.

On the barbecue were the newest spring lambs and goat meat that had been marinated overnight in rosemary and oil. Ouzo, Metaxa, Amstel beer and Crasi, the local wine, flowed freely. Everyone ate their fill, dancing until the early hours of the morning. The sun was just about ready to rise again before the last reveller left.

The atmosphere at such occasions was extremely happy, with everyone making Ruth and Joe very welcome.

They knew that they had been accepted by the village people.

CHANGING TIMES

Niso had a family who still lived in Australia. During the summer, his daughter came to stay with her father at the apartment next to Ruth and Joe's. Marianne was a very attractive girl with dark hair and eyes. A lovely suntan enhanced her good looks. She had a well-developed figure for a young girl of fifteen, which she showed off to its full advantage. She certainly caused a stir in the quiet village among the boys, who seldom saw the other village girls, and certainly never saw them showing so much bare flesh.

Motorbikes were constantly driven slowly past the apartment where Marianne would lounge around sunbathing. The older women of the village were ready to show their disapproval whenever Ruth called at the cafe to see Sula.

A few months later, Marianne's brother joined the family from Australia. He was quite dashing, but the other Greek boys all had good looks so he did not stand out as much as his sister.

When Ruth and Joe were sitting on their balcony, the other two would join them and sit talking in English. It made a nice change for Ruth and Joe to hear their native tongue, even though it was with an Australian accent. They also made friends with an American lady who was married to a Greek. Her name was Alison, and she lived in the village not far from where they had the apartment. Alison had three children, two girls and one boy. They ran a restaurant in one of the tourist areas. Alison was always glad to see Ruth and Joe, making them extremely welcome whenever they were passing. She told them on one visit that they were opening a bakery business in the town and selling the restaurant, as the hours were too long. Her parents were due to come over from America to look after the children whilst they got the business ready for customers.

Alison brought her parents to see Ruth and Joe at their house to introduce them. They were a lovely couple, but a little older than Ruth had expected. She thought it was going to be hard work for them to control the three children, having seen for herself that they were a little difficult to handle. The grandma would call on her way home from the shop for a coffee at Ruth's home.

"I'm glad of a little respite from my daily battle," she would say. On one occasion it was grandpa who came instead. He was very worried, as he did not know where his wife was. Joe asked him a few details and then he jumped on his bike to go and search for the old lady. She was found eventually in the church, asking for forgiveness for shouting at the naughty children.

The final day for the opening of the new bakery had arrived. Ruth and her husband received an official invitation to see the papa bless the business. Quite a number of Alison's friends were present from the village, so there were plenty of friendly faces known to Ruth and Joe. The papa performed the ceremony, which was followed by everyone's good wishes for a successful business venture, then a toast. Alison was having her home built above the bakery and that meant that she would no longer live in the village, much to the disappointment of Ruth and Joe.

They decided, however, that they would call at the bakery as often as they could when they were in the town, for a chat.

The shop had only been open a few days when they decided to pay a visit. Much to their dismay, they found Alison with a very dirty face and hands and the shop covered with black burnt surfaces. There had been an arson attempt during the night. They had managed to put out the blaze, but not before it had done quite a lot of damage and smoke had affected most of the shop area. They would have to close down until the mess could be cleaned up and the shop refurbished again.

Alison had a good idea who had done it, as their baker had worked for someone else and left there to go and work for her. She had no proof of this, of course, so she could do nothing about it.

"We will start again," she told them. "This sort of thing can happen between rivals here in Greece."

The summer holidays were beginning for the Greek people in

Athens. Most of them wanted to escape the smog and the heat caused by traffic during the height of summer, so they made their way across the water to the islands where there was always a gentle refreshing breeze blowing from the sea.

Niso had been building rented rooms underneath the apartment for quite some time with the main purpose of renting them out to the Greeks. Unfortunately, he was having to turn people away because he had not got them ready in time. His son was not too happy about this as Ruth and Joe were living in an apartment that had three bedrooms. He was unable to see that they had paid all year for this and would continue to do so again. He did not realise that it was better to rent for a whole year than for two weeks at a time just in the summer.

He began to persuade his father that he thought it was not right, and started to create problems for Ruth and Joe. For a whole year they had lived quite amicably with Niso. First he took out the beds that had been in the spare rooms in the apartments, then he turned off the water supply, creating no end of trouble between them. Next he removed the TV antenna from the roof

One day, however, Joe had to send for the police, as the son threatened to throw their TV over the balcony. Both Ruth and Joe were very worried as to the outcome of this situation.

On a previous visit to the taverna many months before, a customer had asked if they wanted to rent his small cottage. They had been to have a look at it and were disappointed that they had not seen it first, but by that time had purchased furniture that was needed for the apartment. The small cottage was furnished , so they politely thanked him and said they would stay at Niso's.

When the trouble started, they wondered if there was a possibility that they could come to some arrangement about the cottage. After a visit to the cottage, the man agreed to remove the furniture that they did not need and store it in his garage. This was a blessing for them at a very difficult time, so they agreed to rent the cottage from him The rent was much lower also, which was to their advantage. They asked for the police to supervise the removal, which they did. Another beginning was about to take place.

THE COTTAGE

Some Welsh friends had agreed to help Ruth and Joe move, as had the English couple who had introduced them to Niso in the first place. Niso's son refused to let any of them onto his property so Ruth and Joe had to do the removal themselves as far as the gate, which was hard work. The police did turn up and spent their time keeping the son away from Joe and Ruth as best they could, but he constantly shouted abuse at them.

The locals in the village were appalled at his treatment of the 'nice English couple,' Sula told them the following day.

"Niso was to blame - he should have stopped him. Now no one in the village will talk to him," she said.

As it turned out Niso's son had done them a favour, for they loved little old traditional Greek cottage. There was no fancy marble floor or spectacular bathroom, but it was cosy. They had spent a very cold winter previously in Niso's apartment, with blankets wrapped round them in the evening as they watched the TV. The bed had always felt damp and they had used a hairdryer to warm it each night before getting into bed. After a warming bath, they had immediately turned cold again as the apartment was so big and had no heat except for the small Calor gas fire they had bought. This fire would warm the whole of the cottage in no time.

The new landlord, Baptista, was from Athens; he had worked in South Africa as a builder for a number of years and spoke broken English. He was a nice man who had built a large house next to the cottage which had been his family home many years before. His intention was to move back to the island and retire.

His daughter, however, had married unsuccessfully and divorced, left alone with two boys to look after. Her father and mother had to stay in Athens to care for the grandchildren so that she could go out to work. They came to the island regularly for his farm work and for their holidays, bringing the whole family with them. Ruth liked

Baptista's wife and daughter very much. With the daughter translating for her mum, Ruth had many conversations with her. She showed Ruth many little kindnesses. When there was something different cooking, they would bring her a plate to sample. She was invited into their home on a regular basis to watch the Greek way of doing things.

Baptista found out that she liked to garden and together they planted the crops for the summer. After that, Ruth would open her door to find huge melons and tomatoes on the door step.

On the land, fruit trees were in abundance. Orange, lemon, apple, plum and cherry all grew in the garden, which spread for quite a distance. There were grapevines in one area for currants and another side had the wine grapes, whilst nearest the houses the dessert grapes hung within easy reach for eating any time. Geraniums and honeysuckle mingled together with jasmine around the door to the cottage in a small concrete area with a low wall. From the front of the cottage the view spread across the fertile land with pine trees and eucalyptus scattered among the roof tops of other cottages, dotted around the various farms. Over these, the opposite island could plainly be seen. On one side of the cottage ran a ridge of mountains. High on the hill behind, the local village church stood proudly in the midday sun.

This had been Ruth's vision of Greece. One thing they had not reckoned on, however, was the earth tremors they felt now and again. The first one they experienced was while they were out on the bike on a visit to the town. Joe had been a bit vexed with Ruth, complaining that she was not a good pillion passenger on the bike as she was leaning the opposite way to him.

They learned on their return to the cottage that an earth tremor had hit the island. It had happened at the time Joe had been vexed with Ruth, and this led to a conversation with Baptista about the island many years before.

One large tremor had hit and most of the town had been destroyed. He told them how the Greeks had worked to rebuild it, and that most of the town had some part of it that had been built by him. Some of the tremors were mild whilst others were a little frightening as the furniture shook and things fell off the shelves. It was a funny experience for the English couple that they had not encountered before.

Ruth's love of gardening also came to the fore during the autumn months. Baptista had mentioned that he would have liked to pull down the old goat shed that stood dilapidated at the back of the cottage. His wife had asked him many times to dismantle it but he was too busy with his other gardening, which was much more important. He had made a grape canopy at the side of it, so it was not practical to take round his tractor, which would have done the job in no time. Ruth and Joe asked if they could take it down during the winter months whilst he was in Athens.

"It would give us something to do," Joe told him. He agreed gratefully and told them they could do whatever they wanted on the land.

The weather was mild and sunny when they eventually began the demolition work.

"Look at all these bricks," Joe said to Ruth, "they've all been hand made at some time. It's a pity we can't find a use for them."

"I know what I can do with them," Ruth replied. "We'll make a path round the edge of the front garden wall, as it gets a little muddy when it rains. We can make a fancy pattern with them. I think they'll look nice, don't you?"

"It sounds like a lot of hard work to me," Joe replied.

In no time at all the goat shed was demolished and the bricks stacked up in rows. Joe carried them round to where Ruth was patiently laying them into a pattern where she wanted the path.

"That looks nice, love, it'll certainly be an improvement," Joe told her.

The work lasted quite a few days, as Ruth found it harder than she thought. Her knees and back ached and her hands were getting to be rather rough with handling the bricks. Whilst the dismantling work was taking place Joe discovered a snake pit under the ground, but luckily it only had small snakes the size of worms in it. There were also scorpions in the old brickwork, but Joe managed to escape any danger from them. Ruth and Joe had both seen the larger snakes that lived on the island all the time, so were a little cautious after that.

The path around the front of the cottage looked a treat when it was finished and both of them agreed that it was worth all the effort they had put into the project. The roof of the shed had some interesting looking tiles, different to flat English ones. When they stood alongside each other, they formed a scalloped edge.

"We can make some raised beds with these if I dig a channel and sink half the tile into it. With them standing side by side we can make quite an interesting feature, Joe," said Ruth. It was a challenge she just had to try.

Looking around the area, Ruth found to her delight that a lot of soil had banked up over the years that she could use to fill her feature if Joe would help her. Together they began to dig, discovering to their delight some beautiful white natural stones beneath. They carried the soil away from a large patch to reveal a square area just in front of the grape press. Two steps led down from the press and a channel had been made for the wine to flow away into buckets, as they discovered to their delight. Beyond this, a huge concrete slab lay, ending up against the wall below their kitchen window.

They had adopted a pup during the summer months from some English people and had named her Peggy. She was quite boisterous, so had to be kept chained like the other Greek dogs or she would have chased someone's chickens. They had also inherited a kennel for her. While they were gardening, they had placed Peggy and her kennel on the concrete slab along with her water dish and some chews.

The sky began to look a little dark so they decided to go into the cottage and make a much-needed cup of tea, taking the dog with them and leaving the wheelbarrow alongside the kennel. Ruth was standing at the sink rinsing out the teacups when she heard the thunder and saw the lightening. Then one almighty crash was heard and she thought at first that they had been struck by lightening. Later on, going back into the garden, she realised what the crash had been.

She was shocked to see a gaping hole below the kitchen window, with the kennel and wheelbarrow at the bottom of it.

"Joe, look at this," she shouted, "it's dismantled all the drainage pipes from the cottage – they're all down in the hole. What can we do? Baptista will be very angry with us." The hole was where the pit, or votros, was.

"Lucky we'd just gone into the cottage, or we might all have been down there with the kennel since we've both been walking over it most of the day," was Joe's comment.

Baptista was not annoyed at all, as he had made a much larger hoe when he had built his own house. He suggested they help him to dig a trench to enable him to put their waste disposal pipes into his new one. They all tackled the job together, and in no time at all it was completed.

"It needed doing anyway," Baptista told them, "so now it's done, and thank you for your help."

Baptista was elated at the sight of his steps and the channel from the grape press.

"I did not know they were there; that will make my life a lot easier when it is wine time." He also noticed that his old goat shed had gone.

"Great! You managed to remove it then. Was it hard work?" he asked.

"No, not really," Joe replied with a laugh, looking at Ruth.

Baptista had to return to Athens after the trench and piping work was completed, as he had made a special journey to sort out their problem. It would be spring before they would see him again.

After he had left they returned to the garden project, using the broken bricks to make a crazy paved area to the back of the cottage. Ruth began to make a place for a vegetable plot of her own where the old goat shed had stood. The hole made an excellent place to get rid of any stones or tiles they could not use, as well as any rubble left from the goat shed foundations. It was surprising how soon it began to fill. The long bamboo needed to be sorted out, as it was too overgrown. Using some of the white stones, they made a banking to retain the soil in front of the bamboo patch. Still they had a lot of broken bricks left over, so they proceeded to make a crazy paving path all around the back of the cottage until it reached the concrete patio between the two houses.

The job was finally completed with two more beds for growing flowers and a strawberry plot. Standing back to survey their handiwork, Ruth and Joe were well pleased. It had made the whole area look much tidier and far more pleasing to the eye. All the backbreaking paving they had done would make it much easier during the wet season to get to the fruit orchard at the back.

When the spring finally arrived, the family came for a break from Athens and they were amazed and very pleased to see the transformation that had taken place in their absence. Baptista's wife especially was highly delighted at the absence of the goat shed.

All who visited the family from then on were taken for a tour around the cottage area, and all were surprised at Ruth and Joe's handiwork of Joe and Ruth.

It had been a very worthwhile exercise.

BACK TO WORK

It was springtime once again and the tourists were about to return to the island for the summer season. Once more, flights began to pass more frequently over the cottage. Early May was a beautiful time, with the wild flowers in profusion covering the ground in the olive groves. Some tourists arrived, but the weather was a little unpredictable at that time of year as the rain often came. Ruth and Joe knew that the tourists coming later in the year would not see the island at its best, for the hot sun would have dried a lot of the lush vegetation in midsummer.

They decided that it was the time for the pair of them to try for some work for the summer. The Welsh couple they had met the previous year had been acting as entertainers at a beach bar the previous summer, but had decided not to do it again as they wanted to do other things. They asked Ruth and Joe if they would like to be introduced to the owners of the beach bar and discuss the possibility of some work for the summer.

Ruth found to her surprise that the owner's wife was an English girl. They hit it off straight away.

"We have some rooms for hire and we run the restaurant and bar," she told Ruth. "Entertainment is an advantage, as the tourist's are more likely to come to us if we have some," she said. We'd like some help with the restaurant if you would like to give it a try."

They began the following week, Ruth taking the meal orders while Joe attended to the bar. The English owner and her Greek husband did all the catering. Ruth served on tables and in between did some washing up.

The setting was ideal, leading through a small garden area onto the beach a few feet away from the water's edge. The whole bay could be seen from the restaurant; a magnificent sight. The sun worshippers could pop in for liquid refreshments, a meal or a snack without disturbing their sunbathing for very long. There was a covered seating area for if it rained, but the majority of tourists preferred to sit at the tables in the open adjoining the beach where they could still sunbathe.

Joe decided to run a quiz one evening a week. Together with Ruth, he compiled a list of questions that changed from day to day in case the tourists came into the restaurant more than once in a fortnight.

It turned out to be a great success, as the customers from the night before usually came back with friends the next day. Ruth was extra busy serving on the tables, and she also had to run the bar while the quiz was in progress. The owners of the restaurant were kept very busy preparing the meals.

Some of the tourists gave them good tips after a very enjoyable evening, or when they were ready to go home they left all their loose change for Joe and Ruth, who were paid on a commission basis so all the extra cash came in very handy.

Joe had purchased a bike of his own instead of renting one, so he was responsible for the repairs and buying petrol for it. Their tips adequately covered this extra expense. During their free time they would go to the beach for a swim. They called at the local supermarket on the way home for the food they required, which was very little as the garden provided quite a lot.

Usually it was the early hours before the last customer went back to their hotel or room. Joe would get the bike started and Ruth would climb aboard and away they would go until the following day. There was very little lighting on the streets and tourists were advised to bring torches with them at night.

Quite often Ruth and Joe would see snakes slithering across the road in the headlights of the bike on their way home. They always made Ruth shudder, but Joe managed to avoid them each time. Ruth was amazed to see chickens flying up into the trees at dusk, sensibly getting away from the horrible snakes.

The sun and the fresh air had given both Ruth and Joe a fantastic tan by the second year in Greece. They were both very healthy-looking and enjoying their life on the island.

Anthony came for a visit, bringing a girl friend with him, and Joe and Ruth arranged to go and meet him one evening. He had said he had a friend with him who he would like them to meet.

They nearly didn't make it.

During the afternoon they had gone to a beach for a dip as usual. The bike had played up and they ended up falling off it. Joe was all right, if a little shaken, but Ruth was trapped underneath it by her leg. Luckily it was on a quiet stretch of path away from other traffic. Joe untangled Ruth from the bike, inspecting her and the bike for damage.

Ruth's head had taken a bang on the ground and was bleeding quite badly. There was a cottage nearby, but no one was at home. They had a water point in the garden and Joe soaked Ruth's beach towel under the tap. Holding this on her head, she managed to stop the flow of blood. Joe inspected her but decided it was not too bad and would heal on its own.

"Thank goodness," was Ruth's reply, "but I have a humdinger of a headache and my leg is turning black."

Still with a headache, Ruth climbed on the bike to visit Anthony and his friend. On their arrival, Danny jumped out from behind the door, bringing tears of joy to Ruth's eyes. She couldn't believe that her daughter and grandson had come without telling her.

The next fortnight was bliss, with her family around her most of the time. Danny stayed with Joe and Ruth while his parents went to visit Athens on a tour. He was taken to work with them and played on the beach until the sun dropped down behind the horizon. He helped in his own little way to clear the tables, before being dressed in a warm coat for the bike ride home at the end of the night.

Danny wanted to stand in front of Joe for the journey home but Ruth was a little reluctant to let him do this, so she sat him on her knee between them. It was a good job she did, for in a flash Danny was fast asleep. By the time they got home her arms were breaking with his weight. Joe helped her carry him into the cottage, where he was undressed and put to bed, still fast asleep.

When their holiday was over they departed, leaving Ruth realising just how much she was missing her family. It was with a very sad heart that she bade them all farewell, not knowing when she would see them again.

WORRYING TIMES

The summer season turned out to be a poor one for the Greek people as far as tourism was concerned. The weather was good and the hotels were ready, but the tourists did not come to the island in the numbers of previous years. Spain and Turkey were back as favourites; both had been upgraded to a better standard and the tourists were flocking there. There was a much better exchange rate for their sterling and better value all round, as the Greeks had been a little greedy and put up their prices. This was bad for Ruth and Joe, as they needed to make money in the summer to take them through the winter months.

The restaurant owner would not take their advice as regards lighting the area up to make it more visible at night. It was fine during the day when people could see it from the beach, but at night it was a different story. The street lights were non-existent and the entrance to the restaurant was not easily seen from the road. No matter how they tried to convince him, he took no notice but in the meantime his profits were sinking lower and lower as he still had his overheads and the food bill to pay. The tourists were just not calling as they had before, and this was hitting them all in the pocket.

Ruth and Joe's savings, which they had hoped would last them longer, were taking a hammering too soon. The rent and living expenses still had to be paid, but the bank balance was going further and further down. They had expected to be able to earn more in the summer than they did.

Without the tourists, the Greek owners were closing down their businesses and returning to their respective farms much earlier than usual. Joe heard a rumour that one of the main tour companies that had used the island would not be there the following year. This meant that the tourist trade would be greatly affected the following year and job prospects would be even worse than at present.

Ruth spent nights worrying about what to do. Should they take what money they had and return to England, abandoning the idea of a new life while they still could? Should they wait and see if the situation did improve the following year? But then it would be difficult to return, as they would have less money.

She wanted to take all her own things back with her if they had to go. There was many things that she could not dispose of, for they held great sentimental value for her. There were some things of her mum's and photos of her children that could never be replaced. If they had to fly it would be impossible to take these treasures with her. They could return their goods by road if they could find some transport firm willing to take them. She realised it was possible but the cost would be great, taking even more money out of their savings. The English couple in the village had talked many times about taking their trailer back to England for a visit, maybe purchasing some extras that were not available in Greece for their home. Ruth wondered if she could possibly persuade them to go that year and take her things for her. She was willing to pay them whatever they asked, as she was sure it would be cheaper and easier than getting a Greek haulage firm to do it.

She was pleasantly relieved when they agreed that at the end of the season they would travel back to England. The English bar owner in the town also wanted some goods collecting whilst they were there.

When Joe told Baptista and his family that they were thinking of returning home he was quite upset, offering for them to stay in the cottage rent free until such time as their finances improved. Joe and Ruth had hoped that their savings, along with any pay they could earn, would last them until they were of pension age. They had notified the pension agency of their intentions before leaving England and it had been sorted out for them to receive their pensions when they became due in Greece.

Baptista's suggestion was very tempting, but Ruth knew it was a gamble that she was not willing to take. Baptista and his family then suggested that Joe travel with them to Athens to tutor the grandchildren, leaving Ruth to tend the home on the island. They could not both go as there was not enough living accommodation for them together. This was not practical, as Ruth would be stranded without Joe. The bus service on the island was virtually non-existent and she needed Joe to take her to the town on the bike. Ruth was not too pleased about that idea at all.

Baptista and his family had been so good to them that she felt very sad about it all; they were trying all ways to make it possible for them to stay. There was also the dog, Peggy, to consider as she had worked herself into their affections and it was going to be very hard to leave her behind. It was an impossibility to think that she could go home with them, as she would not like the cold weather. Peggy had always been a good dog and was very affectionate to them both.

Baptista asked what was to become of her if they went home and said that his brother, whom she knew very well, would like to have her and would give her a good home. That was one great load off Ruth's mind and one problem solved. Peggy could indeed go to Baptista's brother. He also lived in the village, and Peggy would have a good home for the future, Ruth was sure.

The decision was made that September would be the date for their farewell to the island that had captured Ruth's heart. She should have felt glad that she was going home to her family, but strangely she did not. Instead she felt a great sorrow to be leaving the friendly Greek people who had helped them settle and enjoy their stay for the last two years. Both Ruth and Joe had tried to integrate themselves into their community; helping with the olive picking among the mountain groves and sharing laughs with the locals at the work involved; climbing into bed after a hard day's work, aching all over but very happy and smooth-skinned from the oil that escaped from the olives.

They had watched as grapes were trod with feet to make wine in the wine presses. Ruth had worked under the blazing sun during the day, laying out grapes picked by Baptista, sweat dripping off her brow with the heat rising from the ground. She had done this with his daughter, but only for one hour at a time before taking a break, as the intense heat would have given them sunstroke if they had stayed any longer in the sun that beat down relentlessly in mid-August.

They had scooped grapes, sun-dried into currants, at almost midnight under a makeshift light erected in a rush by Baptista. They had worked alongside Baptista, with his wife in her nightclothes after the tractor had arrived almost too late to do the work. All the work completed by the early hours of the morning, they had laughed their heads off on returning to the cottage.

"We must be mad," said Joe, "but it was fun anyway, wasn't it Ruth?"

"Indeed it was. Different - not many people would have ever done that before, I'm sure," Ruth said with a laugh.

As the days slipped by, the day of departure drew nearer. Ruth received a letter from Anne Marie to say that Tracy had got married again. She had enclosed a newspaper cutting, but it did not name Ruth as Tracy's mother. Quite the contrary; a total stranger was named. Samantha had been one of her bridesmaids. Ruth felt very hurt about this. She had not heard from Tracy once during the whole two years that they had been away. She would not forget very easily the shabby way that Tracy had treated her. She put any further thoughts of her to the back of her mind, but the hurt went very deep.

The packing began in earnest, as the trailer had to be loaded before their departure by plane the following week. The price they would have to pay was almost one thousand pounds, plus their air fares, so the money had to be withdrawn and the bank account closed. Still the sadness persisted with Ruth; she should have been very happy at the prospect of returning to her family and she could not explain why she felt as she did.

It was a very tearful farewell they said to Baptista and his family. All of them felt so sad, and Ruth promised that if possible they would return one day, if only for a holiday. Baptista told them that the cottage would always be available for their return.

Joe had to dash away, as saying goodbye to Peggy was more than he could bear. The family waved until Ruth and Joe were completely out of sight.

It was with a sad heart that Ruth boarded the plane that would take her back to her old home town. As the plane flew over the island that had been her home for the last two years, heading out over the sea with the sun shining on the water and making it shimmer, she said a fond farewell.

The tears fell once again.

EPILOGUE

On arrival at the airport in England, they caught a train to their home town. Ruth was amazed at how emerald green the trees and fields looked from the window of the train. She had never thought of England as being so brightly green, but she was seeing it from a different viewpoint now. For the first time, she understood why the foreign tourists came to England from abroad; it was actually very beautiful.

They stayed with Anne Marie for a while until they were able to find a flat of their own. It was a start and Ruth was grateful for it, though she did not really want to live in a flat for any length of time.

One evening while they were still at Anne Marie's, Tracy visited with her new husband and Samantha, who had grown but did not seem to know them and was reluctant to talk. Ruth did not mention her anger at Tracy; she was saving that for another day and a time when she could talk to her alone.

Ruth found it exceptionally hard to re-adjust to life in England on her return, yet it did not seem to affect Joe at all. She found the people less friendly and she alarmed at the traffic noise, which seemed to be deafening at times, and of crossing the busy roads. Yet all these things had been so familiar to her before she left. The boredom was the worst she had to contend with; the hours seemed to drag each day. Joe was quite happy to sit and read, often lost in stories for hours on end.

She decided to enrol at the WRVS in the town to see if they could find her something to do. She was asked if she would like to help deliver meals on wheels twice a week to the elderly who were living in their own homes. At least it would give her something to do.

After doing the meal rounds for a number of months she was asked if she would also like to help out in the snack bar at the local Magistrates' Court which was run to raise funds for charitable cases, buying wheelchairs for the needy and donating equipment to the local hospital. Ruth enjoyed the work and met many of the town rogues when they appeared at the court on various charges. She also made friends with the clerks and solicitors who often bought snacks from her between cases. Time was passing much faster and she felt that she was doing something useful again.

Anthony came to see her with his girlfriend and broke they new that they were going to have a baby. The couple moved in together and before long she gave birth to a son; a second grandson for Ruth. Ruth agreed to look after the baby to enable her future daughter-in-law to go back to work, so some of her voluntary work with the WRVS had to stop. Joe had begun to complain a little about her always being out anyway.

Ruth loved looking after the child and watched him grow into a toddler. He was a good child and caused her no trouble at all. Ruth would get him ready, and together they would wander down the town. Time was passing very nicely.

Anthony's wedding was a grand affair, with Joe proudly standing in in place of Harry, who had declined the invitation, much to Anthony's sorrow.

Samantha was still living with her father and grandparents in the outer area of the town. She attended the village school so Ruth and Joe did not see her quite as often as they would have liked. Her grandmother called on rare occasions when she was in town, bringing Samantha with her. On one such occasion, not many months after she had been widowed, grandmother told them that she was having trouble with her stomach. Sadly, within a matter of months she had died and Samantha began to stay with Ruth and Joe on a regular basis, with her father's agreement.

On odd occasions, very rarely, Tracy would re-appear and take Samantha out. The child appeared to idolise her mother and Ruth had to bite her tongue to prevent herself from voicing her disgust at her daughter for the way she treated the girl. If Tracy was expected to turn up and didn't, Ruth had a bad time with Samantha, who would fly into a temper tantrum. At those times, nothing Ruth said or did would console her.

Eventually, Tracy moved to another town altogether and disappeared from the scene altogether. Ruth could hardly believe that a daughter of hers could treat her own child this way.

Anthony and his wife had another baby, a boy, and again Ruth took on the childminding while her daughter-in-law returned to work. Ruth enjoyed every minute of her baby minding but Joe found it a little stressful, not having been used to small infants around his home. He played with the children nevertheless, and as they grew a little older he showed more interest in them, reading fairy tales and playing games with the two young tots.

Anne Marie had been through a divorce and settled down again after marrying her new partner. She left her job at the Chamber of Commerce to work for her new husband, who had a business of his own. Ruth was a little perturbed by this news, but said nothing as her daughter seemed to think everything would be alright. The couple worked very hard and built up a prosperous business between them.

Time was Anne Marie's biggest headache; she found she did not have enough of it. She asked Ruth if it was possible for her to do a little cleaning for her at her home. Ruth agreed and spent one day a week doing chores that Anne Marie had no time for. On one of her cleaning days, after leaving Joe sanding a table that needed re-varnishing, Ruth heard the phone ring. It was Joe, who sounded to be in some distress.

"Can you come home please, Ruth? I don't feel too well," he said.

"What's wrong?" asked Ruth.

Joe had pain in his chest. Her nursing experience told her that this could be the early stages of a heart attack. On arriving home, Ruth took one look at Joe's blue lips and saw the cold sweat on his brow. He was clutching his chest and had a frightened look in his eyes.

Joe had had two heart attacks, but fortunately made a good

recovery and was discharged from hospital with instructions to look after himself and take life easy.

The following year Ruth and Joe decided it was time to revisit the beautiful island of Greece again, but on the Sunday morning before they were due to fly out the news came that the Princess of Wales had been killed in a car crash in Paris; the news that rocked the world.

They arrived at a very subdued village on the island, to find that the locals were just as shocked at the death of the beloved Princess. Most of them were glued to their televisions, watching the tributes being paid to her. The tragic event spoilt their holiday a little, but they found that the people had not forgotten them.

Sula came running, faster than Ruth had ever seen her move before, when she first saw them getting off the bike. She threw her arms round Ruth, almost smothering her in her ample bosom. The island had not changed at all in the four years they had been away; it was just like stepping back in time.

At the end of their holiday, as the plane flew away and carried them back to reality, Ruth still felt the magic of the island that had entranced her heart seven years before on her first visit.

Due to Joe's involvement with an association for former member of the Territorial Army, a computer made an appearance in their home. Ruth spent many hours trying out different programmes and found it fascinating. She enrolled at the local media centre in her town where women were allowed four lessons free on the use of the Internet. After her first session the tutor told her that she knew what she was doing and asked her to work with them as a volunteer to help teach the other women.

Ruth accepted; it was something she was interested in and it also helped to pass the time, for she was feeling a little bored once more. The child minding had diminished as the younger children were at school and the older ones were not now as dependent on her.

During one of her volunteer sessions, Ruth was assisting a learner to research her family tree and as a demonstration she typed in her own maiden name. Much to Ruth's amazement, her unusual name showed up with an e-mail address for New Zealand. She stared at the e-mail address ending N.Z and the combination of her name for a long time.

"Could this possibly be my brother Gordon?" she said in her surprise to the lady next to her.

With a pounding heart she sent an e-mail to the address, asking if they knew a Gordon. She did not really expect a reply, yet hoped fervently that she would get one. She held her breath, praying that any reply would be favourable. A few sleepless nights followed.

Within days, a message appeared on her home computer from New Zealand. Ruth was overwhelmed as she read the message. Her eyes filled with tears and there was a joyous feeling in her heart as she read: "Gordon was my father."

Ruth ran as fast as she could into the room where Joe was sitting quietly reading, as he usually did while she played on the computer.

"Joe," she called excitedly, her eyes filled with happiness. "I've had a reply from New Zealand!"

"Have you really?" Joe was just as amazed. "What does it say?"

Ruth handed him the message that she had printed.

"She's my brother Gordon's daughter," she answered, her emotions almost preventing her from speaking.

Dashing back to the computer, Ruth sat down to compose a letter to her niece. She wrote about her visits to their home as a teenager and explained the relationship between them. Eagerly she sent off the message, to receive another reply almost straight away from her niece. Sadly, Gordon had died but he had five daughters, all very excited about her email.

With just a few typed words she had traced a family she had not seen for over fifty years through the magic of the Internet. Her one small message had spanned the years and thousands of miles. At last, Ruth had found some small roots that she hoped fervently would grow as time went on. This was to be the beginning of an extraordinary and moving phase in her life.

The e-mails came fast and furious from New Zealand, gradually unfolding a story of which Ruth had previously been unaware. The older girls, now women with families of their own, told her how they remembered her visits to see their father many years before. They had been curious as to what had become of her.

Gordon had carried on his hatred for her father for a number of years but as he grew older he had talked a little about his regret as not keeping in touch with Ruth. The jigsaw of her father's life and her own was mixed up, but gradually it began to fall into place with the help of her nieces.

Ruth's father had been one of four brothers and one sister, all of whom had lived in the town where Ruth was born. Ruth had never known about the brothers and realised, on hearing this news, that she should have had three uncles and one aunt of her true family. If she had true relatives, why had her father put herself and her baby sister in an orphanage at such young ages? What was his reasoning behind that?

Ruth sent for a copy of her original birth certificate and was very surprised to find that her mother had had a different surname to her father. They had not been married. After some research, she discovered that she also had a half-sister and brother from the union of her father and true mother. Her mother had been widowed with the two children, a son and a daughter. These two were also related to her, of course, having the same mother.

Where were they?

She composed an advert for the local newspaper: 'Please help me to achieve mission impossible,' she wrote, trying to make it as eye-catching as possible. She filled in the rest of the family details as best she could before leaving her phone number and sent it off to the editor with her fingers crossed that it would succeed.

Succeed it did, and in no time at all she was in contact with a man who had served in the navy with her half-brother and had known him well. He told her that her brother had died, but that he had a son who was married and he knew where they lived.

The same afternoon she received a phone call from her nephew's wife, giving her the address of Ruth's half-sister. Ruth wrote a carefully-worded letter, to which she received a reply, and they made arrangements to meet at the end of the week. On the day, Ruth was in no doubt that the lady walking towards her was indeed her half-sister; she was so much like Elizabeth.

From that day, the rest of the details about Ruth's mother's death were revealed. It came to light that Ruth and her father had at some time lived with her mother and the two other children. The older girl remembered vividly the trauma and heartbreak surrounding the circumstances of their mother dying and the way Ruth's father had dealt with it. Following her mother's death in childbirth, her father had not been allowed to keep the other two older children, as their own family had taken them from him. Ruth's half-sister could remember being dragged to a car, screaming for Ruth, and her last memory of Ruth as a child was seeing her standing on the doorstep crying whilst she herself was forcibly removed from the home.

Ruth began to understand a little why her father had been reluctant to recall the full story. It must have been a terrible time for all involved, especially the half-sister standing in front of her telling her all this with tears in her eyes.

Ruth apologised for bringing all this heartbreak to the fore.

"We'll keep in touch now and maybe make up a little for the past," she promised this stranger who was her half-sister.

Ruth's head was spinning. Her father certainly had a lot to answer for, as his actions had affected many lives. He had deserted his first wife, the mother of Gordon, to live with a woman who already had two children. That was the dark secret that had been hidden from her all her life; he had not been divorced. That was the disgrace and the shame he had felt, and possibly the reason why he was so annoyed that Ruth had discovered his first son, who also had a sister. He must have been expecting her to find out many other things, such as how his brothers and sister had disowned him due to the scandal. He had taken his family away to another town to avoid any further contact with his relatives.

Ruth could not help but feel cheated of a normal childhood by her father's actions in trying to preserve his own self respect. Why had he not told her the truth when the situation first came to light? She was sure that she would not have passed judgement on him. What a tragic thing to happen to her father; he must have been incapable of thinking rationally about his dilemma at the time.

She had had so much unnecessary loneliness in her life, for in reality she had once belonged to a large family. The discovery of Gordon in her teens could have been the right time to pursue it further, but that special time had long gone.

Ruth would dearly have loved to sit and discuss the situation with her father but that opportunity had also gone and it was not going to hurt anyone if she pursued it now.

With her half-sister's help, Ruth managed to find the grave of her mother in a local churchyard where it had stood unattended for almost fifty years. She presumed that the stillborn infant had also been buried there, along with the mother of whom she had no recollection.

Ruth learnt that her half-sister and brother had made some effort to trace her, but to no avail.

She relayed all the information she could back to New Zealand and they did the same. Photographs of all the nieces arrived by e-mails, as did pictures of them together at family gatherings and celebrations. One of the nieces was building a family tree. It was all so fascinating, Ruth never knew what to expect from them next. Slowly, she was beginning to feel as though she had known them all their life.

A great family gathering was planned for the following year when she and Joe would celebrate their silver wedding anniversary; her New Zealand half of the family were to take the long journey back to

England to visit her.

What a tale she had to tell her family and their children of an unusual life - the things she had done and the people she had loved and lost, the laughter and the tears of yesterday, her thoughts and feelings, the heartbreak and the joy, the despair almost to the depths of insanity at times - finally emerging as a happy person who was looking forward to what remained of her life and the future of her family.

She prayed that for all of them, there would be no tears tomorrow.